Amateur
Athletics

POINT COUNTERPOINT

Amateur Athletics

Alan Marzilli

SERIES CONSULTING EDITOR
Alan Marzilli, M.A., J.D.

CHELSEA HOUSE
PUBLISHERS
An imprint of Infobase Publishing

Amateur Athletics

Copyright © 2004 by Infobase Publishing

Chelsea House
An imprint of Infobase Publishing
132 West 31st Street
New York NY 10001

For Library of Congress Cataloging-in-Publication Data, please contact the publisher.

ISBN 0-7910-7921-X

Text and cover design by Keith Trego

Printed in the United States of America

Bang 21C 10 9 8 7 6 5 4 3 2

This book is printed on acid-free paper.

CONTENTS

Introduction
Alan Marzilli, M.A., J.D.
Durham, North Carolina

The debates presented in POINT/COUNTERPOINT are among the most interesting and controversial in contemporary American society, but studying them is more than an academic activity. They affect every citizen; they are the issues that today's leaders debate and tomorrow's will decide. The reader may one day play a central role in resolving them.

Why study both sides of the debate? It's possible that the reader will not yet have formed any opinion at all on the subject of this volume—but this is unlikely. It is more likely that the reader will already hold an opinion, probably a strong one, and very probably one formed without full exposure to the arguments of the other side. It is rare to hear an argument presented in a balanced way, and it is easy to form an opinion on too little information; these books will help to fill in the informational gaps that can never be avoided. More important, though, is the practical function of the series: Skillful argumentation requires a thorough knowledge of *both* sides—though there are seldom only two, and only by knowing what an opponent is likely to assert can one form an articulate response.

Perhaps more important is that listening to the other side sometimes helps one to see an opponent's arguments in a more human way. For example, Sister Helen Prejean, one of the nation's most visible opponents of capital punishment, has been deeply affected by her interactions with the families of murder victims. Seeing the families' grief and pain, she understands much better why people support the death penalty, and she is able to carry out her advocacy with a greater sensitivity to the needs and beliefs of those who do not agree with her. Her relativism, in turn, lends credibility to her work. Dismissing the other side of the argument as totally without merit can be too easy—it is far more useful to understand the nature of the controversy and the reasons *why* the issue defies resolution.

The most controversial issues of all are often those that center on a constitutional right. The Bill of Rights—the first ten amendments to the U.S. Constitution—spells out some of the most fundamental rights that distinguish the governmental system of the United States from those that allow fewer (or other) freedoms. But the sparsely worded document is open to interpretation, and clauses of only a few words are often at the heart of national debates. The Bill of Rights was meant to protect individual liberties; but the needs of some individuals clash with those of society as a whole, and when this happens someone has to decide where to draw the line. Thus the Constitution becomes a battleground between the rights of individuals to do as they please and the responsibility of the government to protect its citizens. The First Amendment's guarantee of "freedom of speech," for example, leads to a number of difficult questions. Some forms of expression, such as burning an American flag, lead to public outrage—but nevertheless are said to be protected by the First Amendment. Other types of expression that most people find objectionable, such as sexually explicit material involving children, are not protected because they are considered harmful. The question is not only where to draw the line, but how to do this without infringing on the personal liberties on which the United States was built.

The Bill of Rights raises many other questions about individual rights and the societal "good." Is a prayer before a high school football game an "establishment of religion" prohibited by the First Amendment? Does the Second Amendment's promise of "the right to bear arms" include concealed handguns? Is stopping and frisking someone standing on a corner known to be frequented by drug dealers a form of "unreasonable search and seizure" in violation of the Fourth Amendment? Although the nine-member U.S. Supreme Court has the ultimate authority in interpreting the Constitution, its answers do not always satisfy the public. When a group of nine people—sometimes by a five-to-four vote—makes a decision that affects the lives of hundreds of millions, public outcry can be expected. And the composition of the Court does change over time, so even a landmark decision is not guaranteed to stand forever. The limits of constitutional protection are always in flux.

These issues make headlines, divide courts, and decide elections. They are the questions most worthy of national debate, and this series aims to cover them as thoroughly as possible. Each volume sets out some of the key arguments surrounding a particular issue, even some views that most people consider extreme or radical—but presents a balanced perspective on the issue. Excerpts from the relevant laws and judicial opinions and references to central concepts, source material, and advocacy groups help the reader to explore the issues even further and to read "the letter of the law" just as the legislatures and the courts have established it.

It may seem that some debates—such as those over capital punishment and abortion, debates with a strong moral component—will never be resolved. But American history offers numerous examples of controversies that once seemed insurmountable but now are effectively settled, even if only on the surface. Abolitionists met with widespread resistance to their efforts to end slavery, and the controversy over that issue threatened to cleave the nation in two; but today public debate over the merits of slavery would be unthinkable, though racial inequalities still plague the nation. Similarly unthinkable at one time was suffrage for women and minorities, but this is now a matter of course. Distributing information about contraception once was a crime. Societies change, and attitudes change, and new questions of social justice are raised constantly while the old ones fade into irrelevancy.

Whatever the root of the controversy, the books in POINT/ COUNTERPOINT seek to explain to the reader the origins of the debate, the current state of the law, and the arguments on both sides. The goal of the series is to inform the reader about the issues facing not only American politicians, but all of the nation's citizens, and to encourage the reader to become more actively involved in resolving these debates, as a voter, a concerned citizen, a journalist, an activist, or an elected official. Democracy is based on education, and every voice counts—so every opinion must be an informed one.

Interest in college sports is at an all-time high, and schools are cashing in with multimillion-dollar television contracts for football and men's basketball. Other sports, such as women's basketball, are generating increasing amounts of revenue. Supporters of athletic programs say this money is good for universities, but many people believe the commercialization of college sports has gone too far. Too often, academic departments struggle to buy books while athletic departments build new practice facilities. Of course, class work is the last thing that many so-called student-athletes have on their minds.

This volume in the POINT/COUNTERPOINT series examines current controversies in amateur athletics, including whether to toughen academic standards, pay student-athletes, provide more opportunities for women, and reduce the influence of money in sports. Some people think college sports are great for fans, students, athletes, and universities, and do not want to interfere with their excitement and tradition. But more and more people think that college athletic programs are on a collision course and wonder how long athletic departments can continue to receive exemption from taxes and business regulations while earning millions using unpaid athletes.

Amateur Athletics Versus Economic Reality

The 2002–2003 basketball season was the last for Michael Jordan, who is often considered the greatest basketball player of all time. But fans would not have to wait long for a new sensation to come along, as a talented young player burst onto the national scene. Fans across the nation watched him play in games on cable sports networks, and many proclaimed him to be the next "Air Jordan" as he dominated opponents and dazzled viewers with his spectacular dunks.

However, there were not yet any endorsement deals with Nike or Gatorade for this new superstar. LeBron James was still in high school, and the rules of high school competition said that he could not use his fame to make any type of profit. His school, on the other hand, St. Vincent–St. Mary in Akron, Ohio, certainly profited from James's court wizardry: In addition to money from television appearances, the school team sold out arenas as it traveled across the country. Television networks also made money by showing the games.

With all the excitement this young man generated nationally, it might seem unfair that he was denied any part of the spoils, but that is exactly what the Ohio High School Athletic Association (OHSAA) took great pains to do. James grew up in a family with very little money, and, therefore, his mother's ability to borrow an estimated $65,000 to buy James a customized Hummer SUV with three televisions inside raised many eyebrows. Many thought that the bank would not have made the loan if it did not think that James would be able to pay back the money when he joined the National Basketball Association (NBA). The OHSAA accused James of capitalizing on his fame, which violated the rules governing high school basketball in Ohio. The organization made the same type of accusations when a sporting goods store gave James two "throwback jerseys," worth a total of about $800.

Ultimately, the OHSAA cleared James of any wrongdoing related to the SUV that his mother said was an eighteenth-birthday present. However, the governing body declared the young athlete ineligible to compete because he had accepted the throwback jerseys, which it considered compensation for helping to promote the sporting goods store. James took the matter to court, and a judge held that OHSAA could not declare James ineligible but imposed a two-game suspension.

- **Should an athlete from a poor family have fewer "toys" than one from a rich family?**

LeBron James's ability to attract television viewers, and his being beset by people who were more than willing to throw money his way, was unusual only in that he was still a high school student when all this happened. Each year, hundreds of college athletes receive national attention, particularly in sports such as football and men's basketball, the so-called big-time college sports. Other college sports also generate a buzz, including women's basketball, men's hockey, and women's volleyball. Although many outstanding college athletes receive scholarships that pay tuition, room and board, and expenses, universities are

Association: LeBron James Forfeited His Amateur Status

COLUMBUS, Ohio—The Ohio High School Athletic Association has completed an investigation centering on the eligibility of Akron St. Vincent–St. Mary senior basketball player LeBron James. Commissioner Clair Muscaro has announced that a violation of the OHSAA amateur bylaws has been found, and, therefore, has ruled James ineligible insofar as his amateur status is concerned for the remainder of his high school career. In addition, St. Vincent–St. Mary must forfeit its game against Akron Buchtel (Sunday, January 26) since James played in the contest after he forfeited his amateur status. Officials at the school were notified of the decision today.

The investigation centered around published reports that on January 25 two pieces of clothing with an approximate retail value of $850 were allegedly given directly to James at no cost by a merchant in exchange for his posing for pictures that are to be hung on the store's walls. Muscaro became aware of the situation on January 30.

"In talking with the store's personnel, I was able to confirm that on January 25 the merchant gave the clothing directly to LeBron at no cost," Muscaro said. "Accordingly, this is a direct violation of the OHSAA bylaws on amateurism, because, in fact, LeBron did capitalize on athletic fame by receiving these gifts."

Muscaro said there was a significant difference between this situation and his January 27 ruling in which James was not found in violation of the OHSAA bylaws on amateurism when a vehicle was allegedly given to him by his mother.

"The distinction is clear," Muscaro said. "The written documentation I have on the vehicle in question in my first ruling confirms that it was financed and purchased by LeBron's mother alone. The purchase of the vehicle by Mrs. James did not violate our bylaws as currently written. In this current situation with the merchandise, the evidence I have establishes that there was no purchase. That is clearly a violation of our amateur bylaws."

Source: Press Release, Ohio High School Athletic Association, "OHSAA Rules James Ineligible for Violating Amateur Bylaws" (January 31, 2003). Available online at http://www.ohsaa.org/news/sports/news0131.htm.

not allowed to pay athletes for their performance or provide them with any other type of benefit. Additionally, college athletes are not allowed to take any benefits or loans from other people, such as fans or sports agents, or accept any type of endorsement deals.

• **Should television networks televise high school games? Does it put too much pressure on young people?**

Amateurism in Principle and in Practice

The reason for these restrictions in college (and high school) sports is the desire to maintain amateurism. The National Collegiate Athletic Association (NCAA), which is the largest organizing body for college athletics in the United States, employs the following "Principle of Amateurism":

> Student-athletes shall be amateurs in an intercollegiate sport, and their participation should be motivated primarily by education and by the physical, mental and social benefits to be derived. Student participation in intercollegiate athletics is an avocation, and student-athletes should be protected from exploitation by professional and commercial enterprises.[1]

Any payments to athletes are therefore banned by the NCAA and other amateur athletic bodies, such as the Amateur Athletic Union (AAU), which organizes competitions for elementary and high school students as well as adults playing sports as a hobby. The NCAA and AAU also ban "capitalizing on athletic fame,"[2] the offense of which LeBron James was accused. Until recently, competition in the Olympic Games was also limited to amateur athletes, but it is now open to people who make their living as athletes.

With the Olympic movement's abandonment of amateurism requirements, many Americans have begun to wonder whether the principle is still relevant in today's society. Modern ideals of amateurism in the United States are traced not to the early

Olympics in ancient Greece, but to the British aristocracy. As described by sociology professors Allen Sack and Ellen Staurowsky, "As the owners of large country estates, the British ruling class had a great deal of time for leisure pursuits [such as] outdoor sports and recreations. Consistent with amateur predilections, the British aristocrat tried to do everything well but generally avoided professional drill and methodical instruction." [3]

The ideal of amateurism in British society was elitist; in fact, rowing clubs in nineteenth-century Great Britain disqualified not only people who competed in sports for money, but anyone who earned a living through manual labor (and who might therefore have advantages in strength and endurance). Sack and Staurowsky write that, even after the so-called mechanics clause was repealed, amateurism rules continued to discriminate against the poor: "The question was how a world-class athlete was supposed to train, travel, and still find time to work at a regular job." [4] Critics say that athletics should be open to everyone, regardless of family background, and, therefore, it is unfair to limit or deny compensation to athletes whose families need money.

- **Are British ideals of amateurism relevant in the United States today?**

The "Mechanics Clause" Enacted by the Amateur Athletic Association (UK) in the 1860s

An amateur is a person who has never competed in an open competition, or for public money, or for admission money, and who has never at any period of his life taught or assisted in the pursuit of athletic exercise as a means of livelihood, or is a mechanic, artisan, or labourer.

Source: Sara Lee Keller-Smith and Sherri A. Affrunti, "Going for the Gold: The Representation of Olympic Athletes," *Villanova Sports and Entertainment Law Journal 3*, no. 2 (1996).

In reality, college sports are not "amateur" in the purest sense of the term; a college athlete does not have to worry about a place to live or where his or her next meal will come from. In the United States, many universities have instituted something of a modified amateurism, allowing athletic scholarships as compensation for athletic participation. Schools in the NCAA's Division I, which is the highest level of competition, are allowed to award a significant number of "full rides" to athletes in order to induce them to compete. However, the NCAA does limit any payments to athletes, and so a young football star's parents might continue to live in poverty, even as millions of television viewers watch their son play in the Rose Bowl.

LeBron James will never play college basketball like Michael Jordan did at the start of his career. Although James was a good student, he decided not to wait for the money he could make as a professional athlete. Like Kobe Bryant, Kevin Garnett, and other young superstars, he declared himself eligible for the NBA draft straight out of high school. Other football and basketball players have entered professional drafts after only one, two, or three years of college, before completing their degrees. Although many people criticize such decisions, others say that we cannot blame athletes for abandoning their education when millions of dollars await.

- **Should the NBA prevent high schoolers from entering the draft?**

Should Athletes Share in the Spoils?

More and more people are suggesting an alternate approach—paying college athletes a salary. College football and men's basketball earn the NCAA membership hundreds of millions of dollars each year, through television contracts, ticket sales, school merchandise, and sponsorship deals. The financial value of college sports has skyrocketed in recent decades, making some college sports even more lucrative than many professional sports. Given the money involved in college sports, many say that limiting college athletes to scholarships rather than salaries amounts to exploitation.

However, paying college athletes raises a number of concerns, and not just among people who think that it would go against amateur ideals and the nostalgic notion of the "old college try." Universities do not always turn a profit from their athletic programs: The revenue from college football, men's basketball, and smaller-scale sports often disappears quickly because sports teams are expensive to maintain. As a result, some universities might struggle to pay athletes, and those universities would quickly lose their ability to recruit talented athletes. Another important question is whether to pay athletes in nonrevenue sports such as gymnastics, wrestling, and field hockey. These athletes work just as hard but do not bring in revenue, so paying them would be a more difficult question.

Many female athletes are not concerned with getting paid a salary but are more interested in getting universities to offer them athletic opportunities on par with those offered to men. Historically, colleges offered little in the way of sports teams for women, and although a federal law passed in 1972 requires equal opportunities for men and women, male athletes still vastly outnumber female athletes, and spending on women's athletics is much lower than that for men's. Some say that aggressive "selling" of college sports could help provide enough money so that every woman who wanted to could compete. But others say that there will never be enough money to elevate women's athletics to the same level as men's athletics—it is men's athletics that generates most of the revenue.

On the other hand, it is also men's athletics, especially football, that consumes most of the money. Many college football squads have almost one hundred players, even though professional teams get by with just over fifty. The equipment, training facilities, and stadiums for football are also extremely expensive. The question of revenue and traditions are weighed against equal opportunity in the ongoing debate over college football. Some criticize it as wasteful, while others maintain that college football is an important tradition and that it is an important part of the overall "college experience."

- **Does fan interest in men's sports justify spending more on them than on women's sports?**

Unfortunately, many college athletes never have a meaningful college experience because schools view them as players needed to help the team win, rather than as students. Student-athletes in revenue-generating sports, such as football and men's basketball, are frequently accepted into college even though their test scores and grades are well below those of their classmates. Their academic unpreparedness is reflected in their low graduation rates. Do people who are not academically qualified for college benefit in any way from receiving scholarships, or are they merely being exploited by a university that is hungry for athletic success? Some say the answer is to tighten academic standards, while others say doing so would deny many people—particularly those from low-income households—the opportunity to attend college.

Huge television contracts, deals with shoe manufacturers, and corporate sponsorship of bowl games have forced universities to reexamine the role of their athletic programs. Some people believe that the ideal of the amateur athlete is no longer relevant in today's society, while others think that universities must rein in big-time sports. Calls for paying athletes are growing louder, but women athletes continue to struggle for equal opportunities to compete. Big-time college sports bring in big money, but with this money has come intense controversy.

High-Profile Athletic Programs Benefit Universities

A s the 2000 college football season drew to a close, two teams in Florida—the University of Miami and Florida State University—were arguing over which team should be named national champion. The Florida State Seminoles' only loss was to the Miami Hurricanes, and both teams were filled with talented athletes. However, in arguing over who should be number one, the cross-state rivals overlooked the undefeated Oklahoma Sooners. Though the Sooners were undefeated, they competed in the Big Twelve, a conference in which teams tended to play more conservatively and rely less on speed and flashy offense. Oklahoma had won six national championships, but the sport of college football had changed radically since the Sooners' last title in 1985. Most people predicted that the speedy Seminoles would overwhelm the Sooners when the two teams met in the Orange Bowl.

However, Oklahoma surprised everyone—other than the team's faithful fans—by completely shutting down Florida State's offense and winning the game 13–2. The win clinched the Sooners' seventh national championship and returned the team to the national spotlight. The Sooners rode the wave of success, recruiting talented football players for the team. However, with its newfound momentum, the athletic department also decided to give back to the university. In April 2002, the athletic department launched a campaign to raise $1 million for the school's libraries, starting out with a $250,000 gift generated from sales of athletic apparel. The university's president, David Boren, said: "[This partnership] symbolizes the shared commitment to excellence of our entire university family. It underlines our goal of encouraging our student athletes to participate in the academic life of the institution, which is the central focus of the university experience."[5]

Though much of the revenue generated by college athletics stays within the universities' athletic departments, supporters of high-profile athletic programs say that athletic teams' success extends far beyond the locker room. Many people credit athletic success with enhancing a university's overall profile around the nation, raising student and alumni interest, and—like the Oklahoma Sooners—adding to the university's bottom line.

- **Do athletics play a role in how you view universities?**

Successful athletic programs increase universities' visibility.

It cannot be disputed that college athletics bring a great deal of attention to certain universities. Critics of college athletics discount this attention, focusing on the negative publicity caused by problems such as recruiting scandals and athlete misconduct, and dismissing any positive press as boosting only the athletic programs. However, supporters of college athletics firmly believe that a strong athletic program can boost the university's overall image. Some might think of Notre Dame as a "football school"—the Fighting Irish have certainly won their share of championships—but the university is highly respected for its academic achievement as well. The university was one of the first to send its football team traveling nationwide, generating fan support throughout the United States. Though its academic success does not depend on its football team's success per se, it is difficult to say whether Notre Dame would have achieved its stature without the goodwill that the football team has generated nationwide.

Duke University is another example of a school that has achieved a top-notch reputation both athletically and academically. The university is frequently ranked academically alongside Ivy League institutions and other elite schools, and its men's basketball team has consistently had winning seasons and has played in the Final Four numerous times. Coach Mike Krzyzewski likes to think that at least part of the university's stellar national reputation can be attributed to the successful Blue Devil basketball teams. He writes: "Duke's basketball program is renowned for producing a winning team year after year. . . . That kind of consistency . . . engenders pride. Even people outside the basketball program become more prominent because of their association with Duke University."[6]

> • **Do college teams generate the same loyalty as professional teams?**

Duke's crosstown rival, the University of North Carolina at Chapel Hill, has also maintained a reputation for excellence both on the court and in academic circles. Michael Jordan's alma mater has legions of loyal fans, both inside and outside of the university community. Lifelong fan and social scientist Thad Williamson conducted an in-depth survey of more than six hundred Tar Heel basketball fans; his research suggests that the team's perennial success might play a role in the university's ability to recruit not only athletes but also talented students

Universities Excelling Both in Academics and in Athletics

Duke University, Durham, North Carolina (Ranked #4—tie among national universities by *U.S. News & World Report*.)

- Winner of back-to-back NCAA men's basketball championships and finishing second three times during the 1990s; perennial powerhouse playing in the Atlantic Coast Conference (ACC), one of basketball's toughest.

Stanford University, Palo Alto, California (Ranked #4—tie.)

- Winner of nine straight Sears' Directors Cups for top overall athletic program, based upon performance in multiple sports; alma mater of sports legends John Elway and Tiger Woods, among many others.

University of Notre Dame, South Bend, Indiana (Ranked #18—tie.)

- Home of the most storied college football program in history; winner of several national championships and numerous bowl games.

Georgetown University, Washington, D.C. (Ranked #24.)

- Men's basketball champions in 1984; alma mater of NBA greats Patrick Ewing, Alonzo Mourning, and Allan Iverson.

University of California—Los Angeles (Ranked #25—tie.)

- Winner of ten men's basketball championships during a twelve-year span; consistently strong football and basketball teams.

University of Michigan, Ann Arbor (Ranked # 25—tie.)

- Big Ten football powerhouse and frequent Rose Bowl participant; reached basketball finals twice during the 1990s.

University of North Carolina—Chapel Hill (Ranked #28—tie.)

- Perennial ACC basketball powerhouse; won championships in 1982 and 1993 and produced superstars Michael Jordan, Rasheed Wallace, and Vince Carter.

Source: *http://www.usnews.com/usnews/edu/college/rankings/brief/natudoc/tier1/ t1natudoc_brief.php*.

generally. The university has a selective admission process, meaning that many more students apply than there are places available; the university therefore tries to recruit academically gifted students. According to Williamson's research, the average age at which the UNC graduates who participated in the survey began following the Tar Heels was twelve[7]—strongly implying that a loyalty to UNC athletics developed in youth can add to the desire to attend the university. Therefore, it can be surmised that athletics helps the school to attract the talented students it seeks.

Even schools that do not regularly win championships realize the value that a Division I sports program can have for the university's overall image. For example, the athletic program of Tulane University in New Orleans has been less than successful in national competition, and the university considered scrapping its Division I affiliation. After a period of controversy, the board of directors voted to maintain a Division I program, and university president Scott S. Cowen remarked: "It is a time for us to come together as a single community in pursuit of a single goal: the advancement of Tulane University as a world-class institution that is proud of its role as a leader in higher education and as a citizen of its community."[8]

Similarly, Florida A&M University, a historically African-American university located in Tallahassee, has used a national television contract and a proposed move to Division I athletics as a way of increasing its national profile, thus allowing it to recruit talented students from around the nation. In a press release by the university's athletic department touting the university's television contract with Urban Broadcasting Company, a national cable network appealing to a multicultural market, athletic director J.R.E. Lee III noted: "The additional exposure Florida A&M will receive from this agreement will also enhance the image of the entire university. The expansive scope of this package will allow us to penetrate into markets that athletics and the university had not been exposed to."[9] An official with the cable network added, "Our ultimate goal is to take Black College Sports to the next level.

With this agreement also comes the opportunity to highlight key academic programs and telecast the sights and sounds of their world famous 'Marching 100' Band." [10]

Successful athletic programs help boost student spirit and alumni involvement.

Another advantage to successful athletics, supporters say, is that team success boosts student spirit and keeps alumni interested in supporting the schools they attended. Duke University's athletic program might be best known for its success in men's basketball, but the athletic department strives to benefit the university community through all of its sports teams: "The mission of the athletics program, ultimately, is that of Duke itself: 'to engage the mind, to elevate the spirit, and stimulate the best effort of all who are associated with the University.'" [11]

In nearby Chapel Hill, sports also serve as a "common bond" between students at the University of North Carolina, writes Thad Williamson: "Visit Granville Towers 90 minutes before a [basketball] game, and you will see streams and streams of students walking together to the Smith Center. [Carolina basketball] is a primary topic of conversation all year long, the fuel of countless mealtime conversations and late-night bull sessions." [12] In his survey of Tar Heel fans, Williamson also discovered that following Carolina basketball, especially watching televised games, helps to maintain a "community feeling" among alumni well after they have graduated, and even if they have moved far from Chapel Hill. He comments: "This phenomenon, of course, is widespread and not at all unique to North Carolina basketball. Visit any sports bar in any major city and you will see gatherings of alumni from major sports-playing schools." [13]

- **Do sports boost school spirit? Does school spirit improve people's studies?**

In addition to serving as a rallying point for the university community, student and alumni spirit can have tangible financial benefits for the university, in the form of alumni giving. For example, Penn State head football coach Joe Paterno has been one of the most successful coaches in the history of college football, with more than twenty bowl game victories and more than three hundred wins overall. He led the team to two national championships during the 1980s. During his career, Paterno has parlayed the team's success on the gridiron into becoming a champion of the university's libraries. Shortly after his Nittany Lion squad won a national championship, Paterno spoke to the university's trustees. In the words of football-coach-turned-congressman Tom Osborne:

> Immediately following his first national championship in January of 1983, Joe Paterno bypassed the customary acceptance speech and instead pressed the university's board of trustees to make Penn State number one in academics as well as athletics, and began advocating for the libraries of Penn State.
>
> Joe and Sue Paterno then served as cochairs of the campaign for the library, which raised $11 million for an expansion effort that would double the size of the existing library at Penn State's University Park Campus.[14]

Paterno recalls believing that football success alone was not as important as success for the entire university. During his speech, he told the trustees, "It bothers me to see Penn State football number one and then, a few weeks later, to pick up a newspaper and find a report that many of our academic departments and disciplines are not rated up there with the leading institutions of the country."[15]

Revenue from athletic programs can benefit the university in many ways.

Some of the major sources of revenue for college football and basketball are contracts with television networks and shoe companies. For example, the University of Notre Dame earns an estimated

$8 million to $9 million from a television contract with NBC.[16] In 2000, the University of Florida athletic department signed a five-year deal with Nike to have Florida athletes wear Nike shoes and sports apparel. The deal was worth $9 million, including $1.2 million per year in cash and $400,000 in shoes and apparel.[17]

Critics of big-time college athletics frequently criticize the idea of playing on television and signing lucrative endorsement deals with shoe companies. Evidently, critics believe these sources of income taint the integrity of the sports. However, supporters of athletic programs believe that this money has untapped potential for universities. Rather than "throwing the baby out with the bath water," some believe that universities should simply put the money to different uses. Some supporters of college athletics have suggested that, ultimately, the responsibility lies with individual universities to put the money to "good" use. For example, in a discussion of "shoe money," Texas Tech basketball coach Bob Knight writes: "I could never understand why schools didn't take over [the contracting] process themselves."[18] Knight and others believe that it would be far better to follow the example of universities that take advantage of lucrative contracts than to let that money disappear.

- **Should schools allow their coaches to make deals with shoe companies?**

Knight, who became a legend during a coaching career at Indiana University in which he made the Hoosiers into national champions, was known as much for his outbursts—including throwing a chair onto the court during a game—as his winning seasons. However, Knight looked out for his staff and the university. He writes: "That [shoe] money went everywhere—to the IU library . . . to a fund I had set up to endow a chair for two great professors . . . and for a number of other university causes." Knight recalls that a former university president told an alumni group that the coach had been "responsible for five million dollars in gifts to the library."[19]

Another way in which athletic programs benefit universities generally is that a bulk of the expenses of any athletic program goes to provide scholarships for student-athletes. Typically, this money is raised from boosters and from revenues such as ticket sales, television contracts, and endorsement deals. As a result, the university receives tuition money for that athlete, which is used to meet any number of expenses, such as academic buildings, professors' salaries, and research. At schools with high-profile athletic programs, this influx of scholarship money can be quite significant. For example, the University of Wisconsin athletic department provided $5.6 million in scholarships in 2003. The athletic department raises money from alumni and boosters by giving preferential seating at games to people who make contributions to the "Badger Fund," which is used to provide scholarships to 750 male and female athletes competing in 23 sports.[20]

> • **Should athletic departments get to keep the money they make, or should it go to the university?**

At another university in the Big Ten conference—known for prowess in football and basketball—Ohio State University's athletic director Andy Geiger tells boosters that their contributions help male and female athletes in many sports and from many walks of life:

> Your contribution to the Buckeye club provides athletic scholarships which benefit more than 800 student athletes competing in 35 varsity sports at The Ohio State University. These scholarships enable them to pursue their individual talents in the sport to which they have dedicated most of their lives. For some athletes, these scholarships are the only available means for continuing their college studies. . . . Ohio State enjoys a rich tradition of excellence—in the classroom, on the playing field, and in the support we receive from our fans.[21]

Because scholarships and actions such as Paterno's and Knight's pump money into universities, NCAA president Myles Brand has questioned whether universities should continue to maintain separate budgets for athletic departments, as is typically the case. In a 2003 speech at the National Press Club, he noted:

> [University] budgeting involves massive cross-subsidization. Research and graduate education is subsidized through under-graduate tuition. . . . [C]ourses in English, math, and psychology help support music and classics departments. . . . Is the next logical step to openly cross-subsidize athletics programs within the larger university budget? [I] believe [athletic] programs have educational and developmental value. . . .[22]

College athletics also have an impact on the local economy, which in turns helps the university by ensuring that restaurants, bars, shops, and other nearby attractions thrive. While deciding whether to continue its Division I athletic program, Tulane University officials considered a report by a professor at another local university that concluded that Tulane athletic events brought $42 million into the New Orleans economy each year—primarily from "spending by visiting teams and their fans." The study estimated an increase of restaurant spending alone of $12.4 million.[23]

Many supporters of college athletics believe that "bigger is better." They point to the excitement generated by college sports as beneficial to universities, both in terms of reputation and financial rewards. Sources of revenue for college sports have the potential to help universities in many ways.

The Commercialization of Athletics Harms Universities

Sometimes, success on the playing field masks struggles in the classroom. That was certainly the case at the University of Iowa when the football team finished the regular season ranked third in national polls and qualified for a trip to the Orange Bowl. At the same time, funding shortages were putting the squeeze on many of the university's academic departments. The editorial staff of the *Iowa Press-Citizen* questioned the university's priorities:

> UI professors held a bake sale to raise money for salaries [and professors] in Russian and math squabbled over meager $150-a-year travel budgets while the athletics department shuttled basketball players to games in chartered flights and prepared a new $1.5 million practice field for the football team.[24]

Despite the rhetoric of athletic directors and boosters, many people dispute claims that big-time sports are good for universities. In fact, many critics believe that an overemphasis on athletics can actually harm a university. They point to declining academic standards as a negative side effect. Also disputed are claims that college sports improve a university's bottom line. The main counterargument is that revenue from athletic programs is most often used for athletics rather than for the general good of the university, and that frequently athletic programs—and even football and men's basketball programs—actually *lose* money.

Universities sacrifice academic standards in order to improve their athletic achievement.

Although a handful of universities have maintained both high academic standards and athletic success, they are the exception rather than the rule. Many universities, including the Ivy League schools and other top-notch universities, do not participate in Division I-A football or compete regularly for men's basketball championships. Similarly, many universities with successful athletic programs are not highly ranked when it comes to academics. People calling for reform in college sports would argue that there is no real correlation between academic success and athletic success, primarily because there is a "double standard" when it comes to admitting athletes. Coaches, particularly those in revenue-generating sports, are usually able to convince admission offices to admit athletic recruits whose academic credentials are simply not on par with the rest of the students in the university.

At large state universities that do not have particularly selective admission processes, it has become relatively acceptable, in many places, to admit student-athletes who have rock-bottom grades and test scores. However, writes journalist John Feinstein, this phenomenon is not limited to schools with nonselective admission processes:

Even top academic schools like Duke and Georgetown . . . make huge concessions in the name of winning basketball games. At Duke, where the average SAT score is over 1400, it is not uncommon for basketball players with under 1000 on the SAT to be accepted. . . . Georgetown goes even further. During the 1999–2000 season . . . four of Georgetown's basketball players had been admitted to school having met *none* of the NCAA minimums in the areas of SAT (820), GPA, or core courses.[25]

> • **Is it right to admit students with low test scores to play sports? Does the university have a special obligation to these students?**

In these top academic schools, the problem of unqualified athletes is largely masked when academic rankings are compiled. Universities are ranked in surveys, such as the one conducted by *U.S. News & World Report*, based on factors such as incoming students' scores on the Scholastic Aptitude Test (SAT) and their grade point averages (GPAs). Top universities with winning sports teams are able to admit a few stellar athletes with very poor credentials without harming the schools' statistical rankings: A few athletes with low GPAs or SAT scores do not bring down the averages too far in a school with several thousand students. In his book *The Last Amateurs*, however, Feinstein quotes former College of the Holy Cross president, the Reverend John Brooks, as saying that the cost of admitting even a handful of students who are not academically qualified is "too high in terms of academic integrity."[26]

Critics of big-time college sports argue that the problem of the double standard is compounded by the fact that universities award a large percentage of available financial aid to athletes, rather than to students who might be much more talented academically. For example, Indiana University professor Murray Sperber writes: "[In 1998] Duke University awarded $4 million annually to its 550 intercollegiate athletes, but only $400,000 in academic merit grants for its 5,900 other undergraduates; the nearby University of North Carolina at Chapel Hill gave almost $3.2 million a year to 690 athletes and $636,000 in academic merit scholarships for its almost 15,000 other students." This type of spending, Sperber charges, sends a message to "prospective students, particularly those from minority groups, that because the main chance of obtaining a free college education is through sports, they should first develop their athletic skills and then their academic ones."[27]

Some people believe that a more inclusive approach to athletics would do a better job of attracting quality students. At universities with excellent sports teams, the star athletes frequently have little in common with other students, and due to demanding practice and travel schedules, have fewer opportunities to interact with fellow (nonathlete) students. By contrast, at Great Britain's top universities, Oxford and Cambridge, athletic competition takes place between students who are at the universities primarily for academic reasons. In their criticism of the NCAA's "amateur myth," Allen Sack and Ellen Staurowsky write that college sports in the United States are not truly "amateur" because athletes are selected and compensated (through scholarships and illegal benefits from boosters) for their athletic performance rather than their scholastic ability. By contrast, they write: "Sport at schools such as Oxford and Cambridge was (and is today) organized by and for the recreation of the players themselves. . . . Sport in British schools was not professional entertainment for the masses. Rather, it was a vital part of the liberal education of a well-rounded gentleman."[28]

> • **Would college sports be as exciting if only the best students could compete, rather than the best athletes?**

Although British and American societies differ in many ways, it is perhaps not too far-fetched to believe that American students could get as excited about "true" amateur athletics as they do about sports under the current system. The Ivy League schools in the United States, such as Harvard and Yale, used to be powerhouses in intercollegiate football; however, they have abandoned this reputation in favor of something more closely resembling the sports philosophy of Cambridge and Oxford. Yet, even without star football players, the annual Harvard-Yale game still serves as a rallying point for students at both universities.

Interestingly, the problem of declining academic standards

The Ivy League

The Ivy League includes some of the United States' most academically prestigious universities, and several of its member institutions excel in such sports as lacrosse, fencing, rowing, and squash. Ivy League schools, particularly Harvard, Yale, Columbia, and Princeton, were among college football's earliest powerhouses, but the schools have since de-emphasized football; in fact, they have eliminated all non-need-based athletic scholarships.

The league's Admission Statement reads:

The principles that govern admission of Ivy students who are athletes are the same as for all other Ivy applicants. Each Ivy institution:

- admits all candidates including athletes on the basis of their achievements and potential as students and on their other personal accomplishments;

- provides financial aid to all students only on the basis of need, as determined by each institution; and,

- provides that no student be required to engage in athletic competition as a condition of receiving financial aid.

The league considers athletics a crucial part of the overall university experience, rather than simply providing entertainment for students and the general public. According to the league's Website:

might apply to the student body in general, not just to student-athletes. Supporters of big-time college athletics frequently claim that athletic success enhances a university's ability to attract quality students. To test this claim, economist Andrew Zimbalist analyzed data from a number of Division I-A schools over a period of fifteen years. He writes: "The tests revealed that, while there was some tendency for athletic success to increase applications, there was no significant relationship between various measures of athletic success (win percent in football

This successful competition in Division I national athletics is achieved by approaching athletics as a key part of the student's regular undergraduate experience: with rigorous academic standards, the nation's highest four-year graduation rates (the same as those for nonathletes), and without athletics scholarships. Ivy athletic programs receive multimillion-dollar institutional support as part of each institution's overall academic programs, independent of win-loss or competitive records and together with extensive programs of intramural and recreational athletics.

The Ivy League's eight member institutions are:

- Brown University, Providence, Rhode Island

- Columbia University, New York, New York

- Cornell University, Ithaca, New York

- Dartmouth College, Hanover, New Hampshire

- Harvard University, Cambridge, Massachusetts

- University of Pennsylvania, Philadelphia, Pennsylvania

- Princeton University, Princeton, New Jersey

- Yale University, New Haven, Connecticut

Sources: *http://www.ivyleaguesports.com/whatisivy/index.asp; http://www.ivyleaguesports.com/admission-statement.asp.*

and basketball, appearance in postseason tournaments or bowls, [and] ranking in AP polls . . .) and average school SAT scores. . . ." Zimbalist cautioned against schools reading too much into his conclusion that athletic success led to increased applications: "[The correlation] means that poor athletic performance will lead to fewer applications. Thus, this is a risky strategy for a school to follow."[29] Zimbalist's research suggests that the type of students impressed by athletic success might not be the type of students who contribute to the school's academic environment.

- **Do winning sports teams provide a reason to apply to a college?**

Some have charged that big-time college sports might even have a negative impact on students already enrolled in school, distracting students from their studies as they travel to games, camp out for tickets, and watch games religiously. Murray Sperber argues that overemphasis on athletics can actually be damaging to the university's sense of community: "Historically," he writes, "colleges and universities have built communities on shared ideals, discourse, study, and goals among their members." By contrast, he continues, communities built upon athletic championships are superficial: "[I]f Big-time Sports U can only develop these random, occasional communities, then it offers a sad commentary on its achievements."[30]

Critics of big-time college sports also discount the publicity brought to a university through its sports program. Professor and former basketball All-American John R. Gerdy writes: "[T]he exposure generated by athletics has very little to do with advancing positive educational or institutional messages. Such visibility is utilized simply to promote the specific goals of the athletic department." He cites a study finding that fewer than one percent of people who viewed college football and basketball on television believed that the telecasts were effective in informing viewers about the universities or about higher education.[31]

Having a big-time sports program can also have a negative

impact on the reputation of the university in the community. Murray Sperber cites as an example the University of Central Florida's surprisingly successful 1997 football season being tarnished by revelations that players misused university phone cards. Sperber charges: "[M]any years will pass before the public will remember the school for something other than the phone card scam."[32]

> • How long does the public remember sports scandals? Do they reflect poorly on the university as a whole?

Athletic programs typically bring in money for athletics, not for the general benefit of the university.

Critics of big-time college athletics dispute claims that athletic success translates into more successful fund-raising for the university in general. In his book criticizing the influence of money in college athletics, economist Andrew Zimbalist admits that the suggestion that a successful football or basketball team would make alumni proud and get them to "open up their pocketbooks" sounds like a reasonable proposition. However, he writes, "empirical evidence does not support the logic."[33] He cites numerous studies indicating that athletic success does not bring money to the university, and suggests several reasons. One reason is that most donors interested in athletics are not alumni of the university, but rather "boosters"—typically, local businesspeople who love sports. Another reason suggested by Zimbalist is that athletes in big-time programs frequently are not academically qualified to attend the school; he theorizes that the negative impact on the school's "educational/intellectual environment" and the school's academic reputation might reduce potential donors' interest in contributing to the institution's academic mission.

Usually, however, athletic success translates into increased giving to the school's athletic programs, rather than helping the university raise money for academic purposes. Many people who are impressed with athletic success want to share in the excitement by attending games; therefore, athletic departments use the availability of a limited number of tickets to increase donations to the athletic department. Attendance at games is the most attractive inducement that athletic programs can offer, but this inducement is not often used to generate contributions for academic purposes.

The University of Texas athletic department's Website gives a solid example of how athletic revenue is used to benefit the athletic program rather than the university's educational mission. The department uses the football team's annual showdown against bitter rival Oklahoma as a means of raising money for the athletic program: "The Longhorn Foundation allotment of tickets for the Texas-OU game is 20,000 tickets. With more than 11,000 members of the Longhorn Foundation and 53,000 season tickets sold, supply and demand dictate that many donors will be unable to obtain tickets to Texas-OU. To increase your chances of receiving tickets, you may wish to increase your annual gift [to the Longhorn Foundation] to a higher level."[34] Tickets to the "big game" might otherwise be an attractive inducement to increase donations to libraries or academic departments, but instead are used primarily to raise money for athletics.

- If an athletic department doesn't get to spend its money on improving its facilities and coaching staff, would it continue to make as much money?

Athletic programs bring in revenue, but do not necessarily make a profit.

While supporters of big-time athletics point to instances in which athletic departments have written big checks to school libraries, critics charge that these efforts are too few and far between. In fact, statistics indicate that many schools with big-time sports programs actually lose money. Often, it is the universities that subsidize athletic programs rather than the athletic programs that provide cash to help further universities' general educational missions. Although it might be true that football and basketball, especially, provide *revenue*—money that comes in through television contracts, sponsorship deals, tournament and bowl game appearances, or other sources— they do not necessarily turn a *profit*. There is an important difference: Not turning a profit means that the football and basketball programs are spending more money than they take in. This money must come from somewhere, and, frequently, the university must make up the difference.

Professor and former basketball star John Gerdy has actively worked to dispel the myth that athletic programs make money for universities. Except in the rare case of extremely successful programs, athletics usually serve as a financial drain on the university. He writes: "Inasmuch as athletics was formally incorporated into higher education primarily for financial and business reasons, it is ironic that this business proposition is usually a bad one. . . . Except for the very elite programs, rather than generating a positive revenue stream, athletics actually drains financial resources from the university."[35]

• **Should a university spend money on its athletic department, as it does on its academic departments?**

Gerdy cites a 1997 report prepared by the NCAA, which found that 29 percent of Division I-A football programs and 26 percent of Division I-A basketball programs actually *lost* money—a very interesting finding, considering that many supporters of big-time sports argue that these sports provide cash flow. These numbers were 28 percent for football and 30 percent for basketball in the 2001 edition of the report.[36]

Losses cannot be blamed entirely on football and basketball: Overall, athletic programs at Division I-A schools have a very good chance of losing money or having to depend on the university for funding. According to the 2001 edition of the

Athletics a small part of budget

A study released by the NCAA reported that athletic spending is a small portion of the academic spending at Division I-A schools in 1996-97.

Percentage of spending at Division I-A schools

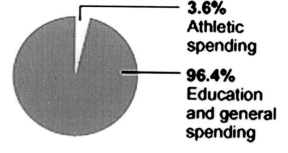

3.6%
Athletic
spending

96.4%
Education
and general
spending

SOURCE: NCAA   AP

Critics of big-time college sports argue that athletic programs are wasteful—that they spend tremendous amounts of money but do not bring in as much revenue as is often claimed. This chart, based on information published by the Associated Press, breaks down spending figures at Division I-A schools during the 1996–1997 school year: Athletics account for 3.6 percent of the total school budget, compared with 96.4 percent spent on general educational expenses.

NCAA report on revenues and expenditures, the average profit generated by a Division I-A athletic program was $1.9 million, but when institutional support—spending by the university on the athletic program—was not considered, then the average amount *lost* by a Division I-A athletic program was $600,000. Approximately two out of every three Division I-A programs reported a profit, but only about one in three reported a profit without institutional support.[37]

Critics believe that big-time college sports are harmful to a university's academic standards and reputation. Worse, many sports programs drain money from academics because any profits are used to support athletics, while the university must make up for the losses run up by too many sports programs.

College Athletics Provide Opportunities for Students

O ver the years, the NCAA has grown increasingly serious about academics. When the NCAA passed Proposition 48 in 1983, raising academic requirements for participation in college athletics, many people applauded. However, some have questioned whether the NCAA should impose tough standards on athletes before they even get to college. A primary concern is that many promising athletes do not have the academic credentials because of their upbringing and because they attended inferior schools. In 1994, the NCAA tightened the criteria further through the passage of its current standards, Proposition 16, and now requires students to complete fourteen core courses in high school in order to be eligible to play NCAA sports.

Among the strongest critics of academic eligibility requirements is basketball commentator Dick Vitale, who speaks at colleges nationwide, urging student-athletes to stay in school and graduate. He thinks that universities should be able to take a chance on people whose test scores do not meet the established standards. In his book, *Holding Court*, Vitale writes that the establishment of minimum high school academic standards "hurts kids rather than helps them. . . . If a school believes that a kid meets its academic requirements and can handle the course load, the student should be given the opportunity. This is America, the land of opportunity, the land of dreams."[38]

Proposition 48 was not an all-or-nothing standard. Some students had the test scores and grades to qualify and some did not; however, some people fell into a gray area in which their grades and test scores were not good enough to qualify, but the NCAA decided to allow them a second chance. These so-called partial qualifiers were not allowed to compete in sports during their first year of college. Some partial qualifiers have achieved academic success. Vitale cites the example of Rumeal Robinson, whose background did not foretell academic success: He had run away from home when he was twelve years old and lived in apartment hallways until a family took him in. He was a partial qualifier when he enrolled at the University of Michigan and had to deal with the pressure of everyone on campus knowing that his SAT score made him ineligible to play. Eventually, Robinson proved his critics wrong, both on the floor and in the classroom. He sealed Michigan's national championship by sinking two free throws at the end of the final game—and also achieved success academically. "Robinson showed them," writes Vitale. "Not only did he graduate from Michigan, but he did it in 3½ years. . . ."[39] Despite success stories like Robinson's, in October 2002, the NCAA eliminated partial-qualifier status, beginning in 2005, which further muddies the question of where to strike the balance between academic standards and opportunity for all.

- **Does there need to be some kind of check on the athletes a university can admit, or should it be up to the university?**

Athletic eligibility provides motivation for marginal students.

The NCAA and universities throughout the nation have been working hard to eradicate the image of the dumb jock and replace it with the image of the student-athlete, who contributes to the university both on the field or court and in the classroom. Some critics snicker at the NCAA's eligibility standards, which, despite recent strengthening, continue to allow universities to admit students with much lower grades and test scores than nonathletic students. However, for many people, meeting the standards represents a major challenge and a source of motivation. Additionally, the heightened academic standards have tended to have a disproportionate impact on minorities: In 1996, the year that Proposition 16 took effect, 26.9 percent of African Americans interested in playing NCAA Division I athletics were academically ineligible, compared to only 6.5 percent of whites.[40]

Regardless of the level at which the NCAA sets its academic standards, high school coaches and students know about them, and, therefore, they do what they can to meet the criteria. Supporters of big-time college sports believe that setting any standards is a positive step because it motivates those athletes who are marginal students to improve their performance in class. It is believed that the eligibility standards do not "bring down" student-athletes with more academic potential, as evidenced by the many student-athletes who excel academically.

- **Is a student who is motivated by athletics more desirable than a student who is motivated only by academics?**

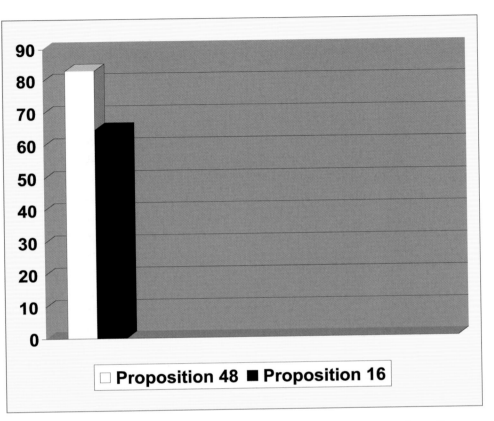

The more stringent requirements of Proposition 16 caused a rather steep decline in the number of college-bound high school seniors who were eligible to compete in NCAA sports. Under the less strict Proposition 48, over 83 percent of would-be college athletes were eligible to play, but under the newer rules of Proposition 16, that percentage fell to 64.7.

With the passage of Proposition 16, the NCAA has emphasized high school grades over standardized test scores. In the opinion of NCAA president Myles Brand, the eligibility requirements for college student-athletes will make aspiring athletes work harder in high school: "My advice to those coaches who are concerned that sanctions for poor academic performance will disadvantage their teams is to recruit student-athletes who are academically capable and to send a clear message to those who have athletic talent to apply themselves to their studies in high school and even earlier."[41]

Brand also believes that the initial eligibility standards will encourage high schools to offer the courses needed to qualify their students for college athletics. In many schools, especially in economically disadvantaged areas, athletic scholarships represent an important way of getting students to go to college. According to Brand, "These new require-ments place additional responsibilities on some high schools to offer sufficient core academic courses and assure academic performance in these courses. This is an example of the salutary effects on high schools by strengthening college admission requirements."[42]

Continuing eligibility standards require that student-athletes be enrolled full-time and be making progress toward a degree; individual athletic programs also monitor their athletes to ensure that they take their academic course work seriously. Tom Osborne, former head coach of the University of Nebraska football team, and now a member of the U.S. Congress, writes: "Players were subjected to discipline and high expectations. Since we believed in the importance of getting a college education, a player who did not attend class was not allowed to compete on the field."[43] At Duke University, Mike Krzyzewski held his players to the standards expected of students at a prestigious academic institution: "Basketball players are simply not going to scrape by in their studies at Duke University. They are going to have to work. . . . I expect every player we recruit to graduate. And I tell them so right up front."[44]

It is not just the coaches who help student-athletes balance the rigors of college athletics with college course work. Because universities often admit student-athletes whose grades and test scores are not at the same level as those of many nonathletes, universities may provide academic assistance to student-athletes in order to help them succeed. For example, tutors help fill in gaps in some student-athletes' previous education. Syracuse University, which won the 2003 men's basketball championship, has a Student-Athlete Services program, dedicated to "ensur[ing] a successful student athlete experience *academically, personally, vocationally,* and *athletically*." The program offers "enhancement of academic performance through the development of study and communication skills, goal setting, stress and time management, tutoring, and mentoring."[45]

Athletic scholarships offer opportunities to many people who could not otherwise attend college.

Rather than seeing eligibility regulations made stricter, some coaches would like to see academic standards relaxed in order to provide opportunities for more students. For instance, when the NCAA instituted academic standards as part of Proposition 48, Temple University men's basketball coach John Chaney blasted the organization as being concerned more with "image" than "the integrity of education," and said that Temple "is not afraid to take a chance on a kid, give him an opportunity to get an education—and that's what I'm all about, opportunity."[46]

• Are there other ways of helping disadvantaged students?

Other coaches take a more moderate approach, saying that students whose academic credentials are questionable should not be barred from enrolling in college, but that, instead, freshmen should be ineligible to participate in intercollegiate athletics. The freshman year could then serve as a "probationary period," in which the potential student-athlete would be able to concentrate on academics. Texas Tech men's basketball coach Bob Knight writes: "[A]nybody, athlete or not, is best served by having a year to adjust to college academic demands. . . . [W]e'd no longer have to deal with predictions of academic success or failure; the athlete would have a year to prove whether he or she truly is a qualified student athlete."[47] Though this idea represents a departure from current practice, Knight's suggestion has a historical basis: Until 1971, the NCAA barred freshmen from varsity competition.

Athletic Departments' Mission Statements

The mission statements of the athletic departments at some universities known for athletic success reflect a balance between athletics and academics and a commitment to the ideal of the student-athlete.

University of Tennessee:

The mission . . . is to provide opportunities for participation in inter-collegiate athletics in an environment that encourages the achievement of athletic excellence and good sportsmanship. We are committed to maintaining a proper balance between participation in athletics and the educational and social life common to all students. Within this environment we seek to enhance opportunities for intercollegiate athletic competition, foster pursuit of academic excellence, support and encourage the achievement of individual and team championship performance, and to be a source of pride for the University's students, alumni/ae and supporters.

University of Wisconsin:

The Division . . . dedicates itself to the mission of providing athletic opportunities to a wide range of students and an environment in which all student-athletes can achieve their academic and competitive goals. The Division strives to provide equitable opportunities for all student-athletes and staff, regardless of gender or ethnic background. To honor its academic mission and that of the university, the Division supports the

Knight's proposal represents a compromise solution that might help both universities and student-athletes who are serious about getting a college education: The university would not have to pass on a talented recruit whose academic abilities were in question, and the young man or woman would have an extra year to prove his or her academic abilities. For many people, this opportunity would come in an educational environment of much higher quality than they might have

educational aspirations, academic progress, and general welfare of the student-athlete. In competition, the Division fosters principles of sportsmanship, respect, and fair play. In all of its activities, the Division insists on integrity, ethical conduct, and accountability.

Washington State University:

[The] Department strives to:

- Conduct all activities with the health, education, and welfare of all student-athletes as the highest priority.

- Conduct a program that is an integral part of the educational system, with the student-athlete as an active participant in the student body....

- Recruit athletically talented students who are capable, prepared, and motivated to succeed academically.

- Provide staff, resources and facilities to support programs that are competitive in the Pacific 10 Conference and the National Collegiate Athletic Association....

- Foster a sense of community among students, alumni, staff and the larger community....

Sources: *http://utsports.ocsn.com/genrel/090501aaa.html, http://www.uwbadgers.com/athdept/mission.aspx, http://wsucougars.ocsn.com/school-bio/wast-mission-statement.html.*

been able to attend without their involvement in sports. The reason many gifted athletes cannot qualify academically for college is that they had the misfortune of attending poor-quality elementary and high schools. For many people, participation in college athletics is their only real opportunity to attend college. College sports are full of stories of people who have grown up in poverty or have come from families that were shattered by drug use and violence, but have had the opportunity to attend college—a privilege not available to many of their peers. Often, such student-athletes are minorities, and it is an unfortunate reality that many universities' student bodies do not reflect the large numbers of African-American student-athletes playing football and men's basketball. However, many people feel that the answer is to increase the recruitment of (nonathlete) minority students, rather than turn away minority student-athletes.

Joe Paterno, head football coach at Penn State University, recalls receiving a letter from a schoolteacher in rural West Virginia. She wrote about a student who was both bright and athletically gifted. She wanted him to have the opportunity both to compete athletically and to receive a quality education. Paterno writes: "He was the only black student in [his high school]. You can imagine the isolation and the constant pounding on his self-esteem that that kind of distinction forces on a youngster in a . . . small town." According to Paterno, the teacher's belief in her student paid off: Curt Warner became a star running back both at Penn State and for the NFL's Seattle Seahawks. As his teacher explained, "But at least as important to me was that Curt graduated as an outstanding student in communications."[48]

- **Should a student be penalized for attending an inferior high school or be given the opportunity to prove himself or herself at college?**

A college education is valuable to the many student-athletes who never play professional sports.

Critics of big-time college sports frequently accuse athletic programs of exploiting young athletes, while providing nothing in return. They point to young athletes who view college as merely a pit stop on their way to the pros. However, even critics of big-time college sports must admit that the value of a college education is quite substantial. For example, although economist Andrew Zimbalist criticizes big-time college sports, he writes that the value of a bachelor's degree is over $200,000 and that "[t]his is part of the return for many student-athletes."[49]

Even many student-athletes who enter college thinking that athletics are merely a stepping-stone to the NFL or NBA soon realize that their college degree will be more valuable than they had thought possible. A shocking number of high school students believe they can become professional athletes. For example, a 1990 Harris poll indicated that about one out of every three high school football and men's basketball players believed that he would make it to the professional ranks; the numbers were even higher for African-American athletes.[50] In reality, according to statistics supplied by the NCAA, approximately three out of every ten thousand male high school basketball players will play the sport professionally, and about nine out of every ten thousand high school football players will play professionally.[51]

Even in successful athletic programs, such as Penn State's football team, student-athletes receive the rewards of academic and personal development. Joe Paterno asserts:

> I watch almost all of our players grow in the game, grow in their personal discipline, grow as human beings. . . . Of all the statistics that magazine writers hang around my neck, the one that means most is that 85 percent of all the players I've

coached have earned college degrees. . . . It counts for more than winning and losing—and I don't care how corny some people say that sounds. [52]

Participation in athletics also helps instill values in young college students, who are usually away from their families for the first time. Tom Osborne writes that today, many young people learn the wrong values, receiving messages from the media that violence, alcohol, and promiscuity are acceptable. As a result, when he was the football coach at the University of Nebraska, he tried to instill values in his athletes:

> Since there is no consensus concerning values that were once commonly accepted, we decided to start from scratch with our athletes when they came into the football program. We systematically discussed values and character [such as] honesty, loyalty, courage, unselfishness, work ethic, discipline, confidence, leadership, teamwork, mental toughness, and perseverance.[53]

- **Does a college education benefit people who are interested in sports, not education?**

In some programs with high-profile coaches, these values can even extend outward into the university community or the university as a whole. For example, after stepping down as head coach, Tom Osborne was elected to the U.S. Congress by Nebraskans who respected his efforts to help his athletes become better people. Longtime men's basketball coach Dean Smith had a similar impact in North Carolina, where he remained an admired figure after leaving coaching, taking part in social and political causes, including the crusade against the death penalty. Recalls Thad Williamson, a sociologist who was raised in Chapel Hill, "I grew up thinking that North Carolina basketball was an exemplar of how to achieve something significant in the world while doing it the right way . . . [partly because of] the social and political values that Dean Smith represented within the state of North Carolina. But the importance of self-discipline also rang through loud and clear. . . ." [54]

Supporters of college athletics believe that athletic competition provides wonderful educational opportunities for student-athletes, and that it is up to individual athletes to take advantage of these opportunities. For many athletes, the desire to compete motivates them to work hard in school, and the ability to compete represents their only opportunity to attend college.

Athletic Programs Exploit Young People, Especially Minorities

For every success story, like that of Rumeal Robinson, who went from "partial qualifier" to University of Michigan graduate, there are countless stories of failure: young athletes who attend school briefly, help the team achieve success, and then leave school with neither a degree nor a professional sports career. Tony Cole is just such an example. The talented young athlete came to the University of Georgia to play basketball but was kicked off the team after being accused of rape. After returning home to Louisiana, Cole began making allegations that eventually led to the forced resignation of head basketball coach Jim Harrick, and the firing of his son, Jim Harrick, Jr., an assistant coach.

In addition to claiming that the Harricks had provided him with money to pay his bills and to buy a television set, Cole charged that Harrick, Jr., had helped him get the grades he needed to compete in intercollegiate basketball. Cole claimed that his assistant coach arranged for someone to complete the course work for correspondence courses in which the basketball player was enrolled. In addition, Cole alleged that while at Georgia, he enrolled in a class taught by Harrick, Jr., called Coaching Principles and Strategies of Basketball, and although he did not attend Harrick, Jr.'s class, he received an A.

Critics of big-time college sports believe that Cole's story is remarkable only because the allegations were made public. They argue that this type of academic cheating is commonplace, but much of it goes undetected. In an effort to win games, colleges admit young athletes whose academic abilities and background simply do not prepare them for college. Rather than helping athletes overcome their educational disadvantages, schools too often allow them to skate through college until the coaches cut them from the team or their four years of NCAA eligibility expire. After they can no longer help the school fill stadiums or arenas, the athletes are cast off and left with little useful training for postcollege life.

- **What can universities do to ensure that athletes take meaningful courses? Do you think athletic departments would allow these steps to be taken?**

Athletes are set up to fail by being accepted into universities where they cannot compete academically.

Too many students come to school not prepared to do the work required of college students and therefore do not perform well academically. As many as one in three students leaves college without a degree, but the numbers are much higher for football and men's basketball players, especially African Americans. Too often, student-athletes in revenue-generating sports simply do not have the academic background or the abilities necessary to do college-level work, but they are nonetheless accepted into universities to help the schools compete in lucrative sports, such as football and basketball.

Young athletes, eager for a career in professional sports, are easy targets for exploitation. Texas Tech men's basketball coach Bob Knight believes that too many athletes are led to believe that they have the potential to earn a living as a professional athlete, despite the overwhelming odds against making it to the NFL or NBA. In the case of basketball, Knight blames the commercialism of the sport, even at the high school level, in which high school students are given media attention, shown on television, pestered by agents, and described (usually incorrectly) as being ready to compete in the NBA. Knight writes: "I hate . . . the way out-of-control . . . summer programs [and] shoe company financial involvement. . . . The worst effect of all this may be the damage done to the egos of sixteen- and seventeen-year-old kids, in way too many cases convincing them that they're far better than they [really] are."[55]

Even before young athletes get to college, Knight believes, they have been led to believe that they do not really need a college education as much as they need the media exposure of college sports, which will help them get drafted by a professional team. At least partly as a result of this type of attitude, college athletes, especially in football and men's basketball, have very low graduation rates.

The graduation rates of athletes in big-time college sports programs are deplorable, in fact. According to the *2003 NCAA Graduation Rates Report,*[56] student-athletes who enrolled in Division I schools during the 1995–1996 academic year were slightly more likely (62 percent versus 59 percent) to graduate. However, the percentages of football and men's basketball players who graduated were 52 percent and 43 percent, respectively. Each year, a handful of underclassmen are drafted into the NFL or NBA, but these numbers indicate that huge numbers of student-athletes are leaving school with neither a college degree nor a future in professional sports. (More than fifty thousand young men play college football and over fifteen thousand men play college basketball.)

> • Should colleges be required to ensure that a certain percentage of their football and basketball players graduates? Would that requirement open the door for academic fraud?

The problem of low graduation rates is even more pronounced among African-American athletes in football and men's basketball. The graduation rate for African-American Division I football players entering school in 1996–1997 was 48 percent, compared to 61 percent for white football players. In Division I basketball, the graduation rate for African Americans was 41 percent, compared with 61 percent for white athletes.

Some critics also charge that universities' avid recruitment of African-American athletes is troubling when compared to the overall representation of minorities on campus. In his book *The New Plantation*, Billy Hawkins likens university athletic programs to plantations—large farms in the Old South where white planters relied on slave labor to make enormous profits. He writes:

[Athletic recruiting at predominantly white universities is] an institutional racist practice because of the low percentages of Black students [less than 4 percent] on these campuses but the over-representation of Black student-athletes on the basketball and football teams (57% and 47%, respectively). If the athletic departments at predominantly White institutions can do such [a] rigorous job of recruiting Blacks, these institutions should be able to do a better job of enrolling a higher percentage of Black students.[57]

> • What can colleges do to correct the imbalance between the large percentage of African-American athletes and the much smaller percentage of African-American students?

African-American Athletes Challenge Academic Eligibility Requirements

[The NCAA uses a weighted scale of grade point average and SAT scores to determine eligibility to compete in Division I athletics. A group of young African-American athletes challenged these eligibility standards on the grounds that federal regulations prohibit educational organizations receiving federal funding from taking actions that have a "disparate impact" on minorities.]

[The] plaintiffs challenge the minimum Scholastic Aptitude Test ("SAT") score requirement for freshman-year varsity intercollegiate athletic participation. . . . Plaintiff Tai Kwan Cureton is an African-American who graduated from Simon Gratz High School in Philadelphia in June 1996 ranking 27th in a class of 305 students. Cureton was a member of the track team and earned both academic and athletic honors as a high school student. Cureton exceeded the NCAA GPA requirements but did not achieve the NCAA required SAT score. Cureton alleged that several NCAA Division I schools recruited him before he obtained his non-qualifying score on the SAT, but that after he took the SAT a lesser number of Division I schools recruited him and such institutions denied him admission and/or athletic financial aid. Cureton, who alleged he lost an opportunity to compete as a freshman in Division I varsity intercollegiate athletics because of NCAA regulations, enrolled in a Division III school.

Plaintiff Leatrice Shaw is an African-American who also graduated from Simon Gratz High School and was ranked 5th in a class of 305 students. Shaw was a member of the track team and earned both academic and athletic honors and was selected for membership in the National Honor Society. Shaw exceeded the NCAA minimum GPA requirement for freshman-year athletic participation, but failed to achieve the minimum required score on the SAT. The Division I school that Shaw entered did offer her athletic financial aid, but she was unable to compete on the track team during her freshman year because of the NCAA regulations at issue here.

[The court ruled against the athletes, holding that (a) the NCAA did not use federal funds in a discriminatory manner, and (b) the NCAA did not set admission standards for schools.]

[The regulations] are program specific. Under the regulations, an application for Federal financial assistance to carry out a program must include assurances of nondiscrimination, which ..."shall be applicable to the entire institution unless the applicant establishes . . . that the institution's [discriminatory] practices in desig-nated parts or programs of the institution will in no way affect its practices in the program of the institution for which Federal financial assistance is sought." . . . [It] is obvious that a recipient of Federal financial assistance need not give an assurance of nondiscrimination with respect to programs in no way affecting the Federally assisted program. . . .

Furthermore, we cannot understand how the fact that the NCAA promulgates rules and regulations with respect to intercollegiate athletics somehow means that the NCAA has controlling authority over its members' programs or activities receiving Federal financial assistance. After all, the institutions decide what applicants to admit, what employees to hire, and what facilities to acquire.

[Although the court ruled in favor of the NCAA, a dissenting judge noticed a disturbing trend.] Buried deep within this record is a statement that is of such consequence that it ought not to be ignored. Yet, that statement has been lost in the intensity of the debates underlying this legal dispute. The NCAA's Rule Change Memorandum contains the following statement:

Low-income student-athletes also have been impacted to a greater degree than other student-athletes by Proposition 16 standards. For example, in 1997, 18 percent of all student-athletes with a self-reported family income below $30,000 failed to qualify, whereas only 2.5 percent of student-athletes with a family income greater than $80,000 failed to qualify. . . .

Proposition 16 therefore has a disparate impact on poor student-athletes regard-less of race. Thus, the dynamics of the disparate impact here are the dynamics of socioeconomic status. These are issues of class; not race. Student-athletes are more likely to be adversely affected by Proposition 16 whether they are Black or White if they are poor. Concomitantly, student-athletes are more likely to be advantaged by Proposition 16 if they have attended schools with abundant resources and are from families that know about, and have the resources to avail themselves of, the proliferation of privately sponsored courses that prepare high school students for the SAT exam. . . . The economic stratification that exists in our society often means that issues of class are either translated into issues of race, or the two are so intertwined as to be inseparable.

Source: *Cureton* v. *NCAA*, 198 F.3d 107 (3rd Cir. 1999).

Academic odds are made greater by the demands of sports.

Many students have a difficult time adjusting to college because of the amount of work involved, not to mention other factors, such as leaving home. For student-athletes, however, adjustment can be particularly difficult because they face a grueling schedule of practices, training, and travel to games. Although the NCAA places limits on the amount of time that student-athletes are allowed to devote to athletics, schools and athletes frequently skirt these guidelines, writes Andrew Zimbalist: "The number of hours per week of obligatory practice is set at 20, but everyone knows this is a farce. Including non-obligatory activities in the presence of a coach, such as informal practice, weight training, tape viewing, attendance at special functions, and travel, athletes can spend 50 or 60 hours a week on their sport in season."[58]

The problem, critics of big-time college sports say, is only getting worse. As television contracts become more lucrative, individual schools, athletic conferences, and the NCAA feel pressure to schedule more games in order to make more money. For example, in the past, football teams played fewer than ten games per season, but the NCAA now allows Division I schools to play twelve regular-season games, plus postseason bowl games. More games mean more travel, which, in turn, means less time spent in the classroom for student-athletes.

In the midst of "March Madness," as viewers around the country tune in to men's basketball tournaments hosted by individual conferences, such as the Pac-10, the Atlantic Coast Conference (ACC), and the NCAA men's tournament, *New York Times* columnist William Rhoden pondered: "When do [these athletes] study? Do they read a few chapters after the game or knock out a paper or two on the road? Do they cram for exams between practices? What's your guess?"[59]

Rhoden noted that while the Pac-10 held its tournament, the athletes from half of the teams were missing final exams. For some of the athletes, playing in the conference tournament or the NCAA tournament meant taking final exams during their road trips, which can only compound the pressure of finals. To Rhoden, the system of playing an increasing number of regular-season and tournament games is out of control: At the same time that the NCAA punishes schools for recruiting violations or improprieties, such as a coach's son teaching a class and passing athletes who do no work, the NCAA gives approval to "placing suffocating time demands on student-athletes." [60]

- **What can colleges do to make student-athletes take classes more seriously? What about for other students?**

In his book *The Last Amateurs*, John Feinstein writes that, at most Division I schools, basketball players generally lack the focus needed to do well in school because sports are overemphasized and academics are underemphasized. He writes: "Some players do go to class. Some graduate. A majority don't. And, even those who do go to class and do graduate chose their college because of what it offered to them as basketball players. Their first priority is basketball. That's why there are so many transfers—playing time matters more than anything else." [61]

However, Feinstein does not believe that the ideal of the student-athlete is completely obsolete: "There are sixteen schools playing Division I college basketball who can call their players 'student-athletes' with a straight face: the eight Ivy League schools, the seven Patriot League schools, and the Air Force Academy." [62] The reasons, he believes, that athletes at these schools succeed as students are not only that these schools do not admit athletes who cannot handle the schoolwork, but also that the schools have a different "general approach" to athletics, meaning that the schools stress the importance of academics to all of their students, including their student-athletes.

Often, critics say, students who do manage to pass their classes do so in name only—the university helps student-athletes pass their courses even when they don't learn anything. Critics such as Billy Hawkins frequently cite cases such as those of Kevin Ross, who was not drafted into the professional league after playing basketball at Creighton University for four years and also had to take remedial education courses after leaving school. Sadly, universities are more concerned with

Did Creighton Deny Kevin Ross Access to Its Academic Program?

[Kevin Ross sued Creighton University, where he had played basketball, after he left school with a seventh-grade reading level.]

In the Spring of 1978, Mr. Ross was a promising senior basketball player at Wyandotte High School in Kansas City, Kansas. Sometime during his senior year in high school, he accepted an athletic scholarship to attend Creighton and to play on its varsity basketball team.

Creighton is an academically superior university. Mr. Ross comes from an academically disadvantaged background. At the time of his enrollment at Creighton, Mr. Ross was at an academic level far below that of the average Creighton student. For example, he scored in the bottom fifth percentile of college-bound seniors taking the American College Test [ACT], while the average freshman admitted to Creighton with him scored in the upper twenty-seven percent. According to the complaint, Creighton realized Mr. Ross' academic limitations when it admitted him, and, to induce him to attend and play basketball, Creighton assured Mr. Ross that he would receive sufficient tutoring so that he "would receive a meaningful education while at Creighton." ...

Mr. Ross attended Creighton from 1978 until 1982. During that time he maintained a D average and acquired 96 of the 128 credits needed to graduate. However, many of these credits were in courses such as Marksmanship maintaining athletes' eligibility than with ensuring that they receive a quality education.

This negligence sometimes leads to outrageous consequences: Longtime NFL defensive lineman Dexter Manley graduated from Oklahoma State University even though—as he readily admits—he was illiterate. Several years after he graduated, he had to take classes to learn how to read and write; his testimony before a Senate committee drew attention to the problem of universities that are wholly unconcerned with their athletes' education. Billy Hawkins charges that such callous

and Theory of Basketball, and did not count towards a university degree. Mr. Ross alleges that he took these courses on the advice of Creighton's Athletic Department, and the department also employed a secretary to read his assignments and prepare and type his papers. Mr. Ross also asserts that Creighton failed to provide him with sufficient and competent tutoring that it had promised.

When he left Creighton, Mr. Ross had the overall language skills of a fourth grader and the reading skills of a seventh grader. Consequently, Mr. Ross enrolled, at Creighton's expense, for a year of remedial education at the Westside Preparatory School in Chicago. At Westside, Mr. Ross attended classes with grade school children. . . . In July 1987, Mr. Ross suffered what he termed a "major depressive episode," during which he barricaded himself in a Chicago motel room and threw furniture out the window. . . . To Mr. Ross, this furniture "symbolized" Creighton employees who had wronged him. . . .

[Ross lost at the trial level, and a federal appeals court hearing Ross's appeal sent the case back to the trial court, instructing it to determine "whether the University had provided any real access to its academic curriculum at all." Creighton and Ross settled the case out of court, with the University making a payment to Ross.]

Source: *Ross* v. *Creighton University*, 957 F.2d 410 (1992).

attitudes are particularly prevalent in universities' treatment of African-American student-athletes. He accuses universities of displaying a form of institutional racism against African Americans: "We have examples at predominantly White NCAA Division Institutions of how the physicality of the Black body has been esteemed over the minds of Black student-athletes, thus supporting the ideology that Blacks are intellectually inferior but physically superior."[63] In Hawkins's opinion, the racist attitudes of university administrators help reinforce this stereotype by leading African-American student-athletes toward less challenging majors and allowing them to pass courses without doing the work.

• Do universities exploit African-American athletes?

The result of such academic indifference toward African Americans, some say, is that African-American athletes are isolated from the remainder of the student body, which further hampers their opportunities for a quality education. Former college athlete Derrick Gregg recalls that, "during a recent discussion with a few of my former African-American teammates . . . we realized that we had very little or no interaction with any of our White teammates off the field. Despite what coaches might claim about successfully integrating their teams, simply because student-athletes are teammates does not mean that they respect and interact well with one another."[64] Hawkins writes: "I consistently watch Black students and Black student-athletes segregate themselves in classes even when other White teammates are fellow class members."[65]

Many people believe that athletic departments are more concerned with winning and making money than they are about the welfare of their athletes. Too many athletes are accepted into universities where they cannot meaningfully participate academically, and the problem is only made worse by the demands of game and practice schedules. Problems are especially pronounced among African-American athletes in revenue-generating sports such as football and men's basketball.

Athletes Deserve a Share of the Money in Big-Time Sports

I n 1992, the University of Michigan men's basketball program
shocked the sports world by taking a team with freshmen players starting at all five positions all the way to the championship
game. Sports fans thought that the so-called Fab Five—Chris
Webber, Juwan Howard, Jalen Rose, Ray Jackson, and Jimmy
King—would leave a mark on sports history. They did, but not
for all the right reasons: The university eventually forfeited the
team's victories in the 1992 and 1993 tournaments because of
violations involving Chris Webber and several other players
(who were not part of the Fab Five).

Webber, who went on to become a successful NBA player,
later admitted that while he was in high school and college, a
booster named Ed Martin loaned him hundreds of thousands of
dollars. Martin later pleaded guilty to federal charges that he was
running a money-laundering scheme (helping criminals conceal

the illegal source of their money). The payments made by Martin, however, would have violated NCAA rules regardless of their source: The NCAA bans any loans or other payments to college athletes because they interfere with fair competition. If payments to athletes were allowed, but some universities could not afford to make them, then the teams making the payments would have unfair advantages over teams that did not. Many payments, however, come from team boosters who are not part of the university, and, therefore, it is difficult for schools to monitor such transactions. Because the NCAA does not consider ignorance an excuse, it has punished many schools for violations like those involving Martin and Webber.

- **Is it fair to penalize a school for the actions of a booster who is not affiliated with the university?**

Rules are rules, and violators must be punished, but many people have begun to question whether it is fair to continue to enforce rules against paying players. Webber played in two of the most-watched college basketball games in history, and the Fab Five sparked a national market for University of Michigan apparel. Is it really fair to say that Webber should not have had a share in the spoils? College athletes have grueling schedules, but they must watch everyone else split up the millions that their efforts generate. Many people also believe that situations like the Webber scandal would be drastically reduced or eliminated if schools were allowed to pay athletes openly rather than in secret; legalizing payments to student-athletes would help reduce the involvement of organized crime in college sports. For these and other reasons, calls for paying student-athletes are becoming louder.

Current NCAA regulations invite corruption by requiring athletes to live in poverty.

The situation surrounding Michigan's Fab Five drew national headlines due to the success of the Michigan Wolverines and the individual athletes' personalities and talents. However, cash payments and other benefits outside of the NCAA's rules are unfortunately all too common even at the bottom of the sports rankings. The NCAA currently bans payments to athletes and endorsement deals with advertisers, plus a dizzying list of "extra benefits" such as dental coverage, excessive numbers of game tickets, excessive numbers of meals, travel expenses for athletes' parents, clothing other than uniforms, long-term disability insurance, meals at restaurants that are not part of a team trip, nonemergency long-distance phone calls, and athletic equipment.

Many people believe it is inherently unfair to allow schools to place so many demands upon a student-athlete and not allow the school to provide the athlete with spending money, or even allow an athlete to work during the academic year. The denial of spending money to athletes hits students from poor families especially hard. Penn State football coach Joe Paterno believes that even a modest sum of money could help student-athletes without leading to corruption. He writes:

> I don't care whether we call it "laundry money," or "pizza money," or "walking around money." . . . All I want to do is see to it that a kid, especially a poor kid, is able to go to McDonald's . . . and buy a hamburger when the other kids go. This athlete, sought out socially by others, is proud. . . . Something tears inside him when he has to make excuses for not going, the real, unspeakable reason being he hasn't got the buck and a half.[66]

Basketball analyst and former coach Dick Vitale shares Paterno's concerns:

> My girls have been on tennis scholarships at Notre Dame. I'm fortunate to be in a position where I can afford to write out a check for them to come home for Christmas. I can afford to send them a few dollars for clothes. But what about all the moms and dads who can't afford to do that? Some college athletes can't afford to buy themselves a shirt or tie or go out on a date.[67]

* **Does having a little bit of spending money eliminate greed?**

Many people believe that by strictly limiting the compensation that an athlete may receive, the NCAA is inviting corruption. From the earliest days of college football, when boosters skirted the ban on scholarships by secretly paying student-athletes' tuition, to today, boosters, schools, coaches, and "street agents" have found many ways to provide money and other benefits to star athletes. Their motives for providing these benefits vary. Often, coaches or members of their staff provide benefits to athletes to entice them to commit to a school or continue playing at a school. Some examples include using a car, and providing meals, clothes, or other items. Sometimes, the coaching staff even makes secret cash payments to athletes. So-called street agents try to win favor with promising athletes by providing cash or loans, hoping to capitalize on their fame later.

Under the current system, illegal benefits make the level of competition uneven. By providing benefits to athletes or covering up academic failure, teams profit from the services of athletes who should not be competing under NCAA regulations—or, at least, the teams profit until they are caught. When the NCAA discovers violations of academic eligibility or permitted benefit rules, it often requires the team to forfeit past victories, or it may put the team on probation, which means that the team may not play on television or participate in tournaments or bowl games, along with other penalties. Coaches are often responsible for the wrongdoing, but frequently, by the time a team is put on probation, the responsible coach has already left the school and a new coach must suffer the consequences of the probation. Similarly, incoming athletes must also miss out on opportunities to play in big games because of past wrongdoing in which they had no part. Many people believe that paying athletes openly rather than maintaining a system that is ripe for abuse would allow for a more even level of competition.

A particularly troubling aspect of a system that denies

student-athletes any payments beyond school expenses is that the relative poverty of many student-athletes makes them vulnerable targets for corruption by gambling influences. Betting on college sports, particularly football and men's basketball, is a big business. For example, Representative Tom Osborne, the former football coach of the University of Nebraska, estimates that people wager almost $5 billion each year on the NCAA men's basketball tournament.[68] Because betting on college sports is such a high-stakes business, many are willing to take risks in trying to cheat the system by inducing college athletes to influence the outcome of a game.

For people involved in the gambling business, breaking the law is not really much of a stretch: Those who participate in college sports betting are in most cases already breaking the law, because Nevada is the only state that allows betting on college sports. Most bets throughout the nation are placed with "bookies" who often have links to organized crime; these criminal ties pose additional problems. For example, a gambler might convince an athlete to help "throw" a game, meaning to ensure that his team loses, while the gambler collects a small fortune by betting against the team. Such cases are probably rare; a more common example is "point-shaving." Point-shaving involves not convincing athletes to lose, but to ensure that the team does not win by too many points. Gamblers make money through point-shaving by taking advantage of the "spread," or "line," on the game.

For each sporting event, Las Vegas casinos publish a line, or spread, which is the number of points by which a particular team is favored to win over its opponent. For example, if one year Penn State has a much better football team than Notre Dame does, the spread for the game might be 14 points. What that means is that Penn State would have to win by more than 14 points, or "beat the spread," in order for people betting on Penn State to collect money. People betting on Notre Dame would collect if Notre Dame won, or if the Fighting Irish lost by less than 14 points, thereby "covering the spread." (If Penn State won by exactly 14 points, then bettors would have their money returned to them; to avoid this complication, spreads are often given in half points—such as 13½ points—because it is impossible to win a football game by 13½ points.) The purpose of the spread is to induce people into betting for the "underdog." In this example, if Penn State has a better football team than Notre Dame does, very few people would bet on Notre Dame to win, but many people might bet on Notre Dame to "win or cover."

Gambling has already taken a serious toll on the integrity of college athletics. A study of football and men's and women's

Representative Tom Osborne: Gambling Scandals Threaten College Athletics

Gambling on NCAA sports has become a major problem. In 1951, CCNY had a point-shaving scandal, and Kentucky in the 1940s. In 1994, a Northwestern running back intentionally fumbled to fix a game. In 1996, 13 Boston College football players bet on NCAA games, and several bet against their own team. In 1998, a Northwestern basketball player was indicted for point shaving. In 1999, two Arizona State basketball players shaved points. This was done to pay off gambling debts. The fix was traced to organized crime in Chicago.

[In February 2003], Florida State quarterback Adrian McPherson was charged with illegal gambling, and of course he owed a bookie thousands of dollars. A University of Michigan study recently found that 5 percent of NCAA athletes that play football and basketball provided inside information to gamblers.

So over 36 years of coaching, gambling was a major concern to me. I was always worried about our players getting involved because of gambling debts; but more importantly, as a coach you had to win twice. You had to win once on the scoreboard, and then you had to win again in beating the point spread.

Someone up in the stands who had bet $10,000 on the outcome of a game that he could not afford to lose was not a casual observer. Most of the nasty memories that I have from coaching, and I do not have very many, had to do with hate mail, obscene phone calls at night, a mailbox that was blown up. In general, most all the time these were caused by situations where somebody had lost a bet.

Source: Congressional Record H2507 (March 31, 2003).

basketball conducted by the University of Michigan's athletic department concluded that "45% of male student athletes gambled on sports and one in twenty male student athletes engaged in activities [such as point-shaving] that could have an impact on the outcome of a game. These findings are serious and indicate the prevalence of gambling among inter-collegiate student athletes."[69] Many believe that forcing student-athletes to "take a vow of poverty" only makes cheating all the more tempting.

> • **Should gambling on college sports be illegal? Is there any harm in a basketball tournament "pool," in which coworkers put in five dollars apiece?**

College athletes are treated like employees rather than students.

The NCAA and individual universities maintain that student-athletes are students first and athletes second, and that they are at school to get an education. Many people argue, how-ever, that in reality, student-athletes are no different from other employees whom the university hires for its own purposes. In their book *College Athletes for Hire*, professors Allen Sack and Ellen Staurowsky argue: "Athletic scholarships have become employment contracts."[70] Many people agree that so-called student-athletes are really professional enter-tainers employed by the university, which leads to the question: Why shouldn't they get paid? The people who tear tickets at basketball and football games, the food vendors, and the people who clean the stands all get paid, so why not the people who play in the games?

From a legal standpoint, efforts to gain employee status for student-athletes have generally failed, as courts have consistently held that student-athletes are not university employees. For exam-ple, student-athletes who have been injured during competition have been denied workers' compensation, which provides payments to people who have been disabled by an on-the-job injury. In one case, a Western Michigan University football player was denied workers' compensation because the court held that the football team was not an integral part of the university's business. Sack and Staurowsky criticize these decisions, writing: "[W]hen this test is applied to multimillion-dollar corporate-sponsored football and basketball programs . . . a scholarship athlete's sport performance [is] an integral part of the proposed employer's business. . . ."[71]

In a sense, of course, college athletes *are* compensated for their participation in sports: They receive scholarships for tuition, room and board, school expenses, and fees. Sack and Staurowsky think that these scholarships have more in common with the wages paid by an employer to an employee than with a scholarship given by a university to a student who has shown academic merit: "[Universities] condition athletic scholarships on participation and can use athletic ability as a criterion for the renewal of a reward."[72] In other words, to "get paid" (receive a scholarship), the athlete must show up for "work" (practice and games) and may get "fired" (lose the scholarship) for poor performance. To many people, the idea of "amateur athletics" has been made obsolete by the infusion of money into big-time college sports, leading to widespread demands that athletes be paid more than the value of their scholarships. Proposals differ as to the amount of payment, from a small monthly stipend to a fair share of the money that college sports generate.

- **What happens to an athlete's scholarship if he or she decides not to show up for practice?**

It is unfair that everyone except the athletes profits from big-time college sports.

Opponents of paying student-athletes have held firm to the NCAA and the universities' claims that student-athletes' athletic participation is part of their university educational experience, and that, therefore, they should not be paid. Critics dismiss such claims as the perpetuation of an "amateur myth" that does not reflect the realities of the commercialization of college sports and that is used simply to justify the exploitation of athletes. It is difficult to argue that college athletes deserve a paycheck simply because they work hard. Though it might be true that college athletes work hard, many students work hard at academics and do not receive any monetary compensation for their efforts. However, an important distinction is that average students do not generate large sums of money through their schoolwork, while student-athletes do bring in money through their performance on sports teams.

A stronger argument in favor of paying student-athletes is that because they are generating so much money for universities, athletic conferences, and the NCAA, the athletes themselves deserve a portion of that money. Even people who do not necessarily advocate paying college athletes believe that the current system is unfair. In their book, professors Sack and Staurowsky maintain that, as long as the current system perpetuates the amateur myth, it is taking advantage of young athletes for the purpose of making money. They write: "There is nothing inherently wrong with paying the expenses of talented college athletes to provide mass commercial entertainment. What can be questioned is the use of the term 'amateur' to set a limit on the kind of compensation that athletes can receive."[73] Although Sack and Staurowsky would prefer a return to "true amateurism," in which students attend schools for which they are academically qualified and receive no compensation for participating in sports, they believe that as long as colleges continue to make money by selling tickets, television rights, and athletic apparel, then the athletes who make this income possible should receive fair compensation.

ESPN basketball commentator and former coach Dick Vitale is more straightforward. He writes:

> [P]ay the players. I'm not talking about thousands of dollars, but why not some spending money? . . . The vast majority of [men's basketball players] won't get a whiff of NBA dollars, but they're still helping produce millions of dollars in revenue. They see packed arenas all over the country. They see their coaches making hundreds of thousands of dollars a year. They see coaches and schools striking deals with shoe companies. . . . They see CBS paying [hundreds of millions] per year for TV rights. . . .[74]

In the opinion of Vitale and many others, college players may begin to resent a system that uses them to generate revenue without allowing them a share in the spoils.

Joe Paterno, by contrast, believes that athletes do not necessarily think they should receive a "share" of the money. He writes: "The football player doesn't object to subsidizing volleyball, fencing, and repainting the swimming pool. He understands how he's used, even exploited. . . . The main reason he plays football is because he loves playing football . . . and he doesn't think much about where the money goes." To Paterno, the glory associated with being a college athlete and the pride of helping the university are rewarding enough to prevent most college athletes from trying to figure out their "fair share" of the revenue from ticket sales, television contracts, merchandise sales, and endorsement deals. However, that does not mean that an athlete should receive nothing: According to Paterno, even the most dedicated athlete "does care about—and resents—the humiliation of being broke."[75] Whether or not athletes deserve a fair share of college sports revenue or merely a little bit of spending money, it is becoming harder than ever to insist that college athletes remain poor while everyone else profits from their skills.

- **Who deserves the money that college sports generate?**

Alternatives to the current system would benefit young athletes.

Sack and Staurowsky think college athletics can take a lesson from the Olympic movement, which "no longer insists that its professional athletes masquerade as amateurs."[76] Today, the Olympics feature the best international athletes, amateur or professional, such as NBA players and National Hockey League (NHL) stars. Before this change, the system was ripe for abuse: Some Olympic events were dominated by countries such as the former Soviet Union, which allowed athletes to make a comfortable living by Soviet standards while at the same time maintaining their "amateur" status. The Soviet Union, which was a Communist country with government control of the economy and no private industry, had no "professional" sports leagues. Therefore, the nation's top athletes were easily passed off as amateurs so they could compete in the Olympics.

Under the old rules, the United States, which has professional sport leagues, was at a competitive disadvantage in sports such as basketball because most of its top basketball players were disqualified from the Olympics for playing in the NBA. Ever since the Olympics dropped the ban on professional athletes and the so-called Dream Team was formed in 1992, the United States has dominated Olympic basketball with the help of Michael Jordan, Magic Johnson, Karl Malone, and other NBA superstars. With an increasing number of foreign players sharpening their skills in the NBA, Olympic basketball is becoming increasingly competitive and exciting.

In the Olympics today, the best athletes in the world compete against one another, and there are no questions about anybody's amateur status. Gone are the days when people questioned the validity of Soviet medals in basketball and hockey because the nation used seasoned veterans. Sack and Staurowsky would like to see similar changes made in college sports, in which academic fraud and illegal payments are rampant.

What they suggest is "a two-tiered proposal for collegiate sport reform that calls for a substantial increase in the number of colleges and universities engaged in truly amateur sport while at the same time creating a 'super division' of sports teams that can operate much like the professional sports franchises that they have already become."[77] In their model, powerhouse athletic schools such as Notre Dame, the University of Michigan, Florida State, Penn State, and others would continue to compensate their athletes through athletic scholarships and perhaps even salaries. However, other universities would follow the lead of the Ivy League schools and not compensate student-athletes at all—not even with athletic scholarships.

This two-tiered model is a scaled-back version of the two-tiered model proposed by *Sports Illustrated* writer and former college football player Rick Telander. In his book *The Hundred Yard Lie*, Telander proposes that universities should be required either to sponsor a truly amateur football team—with no academic scholarships—or choose instead to sponsor a team in a new football league that he labels the "Age Group Professional Football League (AGPFL)."[78] The new league would allow players between the ages of eighteen and twenty-two to compete on professional football teams sponsored by universities. Each AGPFL team would use the mascot, team name, team colors, and stadium of the university sponsoring the team, but the players on the team would not necessarily be students at the university. The players would be paid a salary and, for each year of competition, would receive a one-year scholarship to attend the university if they chose to do so.

- **Would college students cheer for a team of professionals wearing the school's logo? Would it be that different from a team of student-athletes who don't really fit in academically?**

The key difference is that under Telander's proposal, AGPFL athletes would not have to use their scholarships while they are playing football. Instead, they could concentrate on football alone while they were playing in the AGPFL, and they could use their scholarships to attend college after their AGPFL careers (or their NFL careers) end. While acknowledging that many people would charge that his proposal tarnishes the tradition of college athletics, Telander believes that his system is more honest than today's system, in which people who are completely uninterested in academics parade as students. Under his proposal, universities participating in the AGPFL would not have to worry about academic fraud, recruiting violations, or under-the-table payments to players. In reality, the AGPFL is not very different from what is already being done today. Telander writes: "The teams' primary functions will be to develop young football players, offer an exciting game to the public, and turn a profit. (Sound familiar?)"[79]

Other than the few football powerhouses, most universities under Telander's system would not participate in the AGPFL, but instead would play a brand of college football that upholds the true ideals of amateurism. In addition to eliminating scholarships, universities fielding college (as opposed to AGPFL) football teams would play shorter seasons, have fewer practices, and would bar coaches from accepting endorsement deals. Telander believes that this system would accommodate people who are serious about both athletics and academics: "Young men who want to be students and also play football may do so [at a level] similar to the level NCAA Division II and III schools play now."[80] In his system, the college football player could leave school to join an AGPFL team, and an AGPFL player could leave his team for college if he decided to concentrate on academics.

A key factor in Telander's proposal is that the NFL would provide financial support to the AGPFL. Controversial Texas Tech men's basketball coach Bob Knight has made a similar suggestion for men's basketball. He writes:

> Our biggest problem in college basketball is . . . [the athletes] we pervert the process to admit—the ones who are in college only to become pros and take up a place that a genuine,

degree-seeking student could have. . . . [The] NBA should be financing minor leagues that would be open to those kids. The whole college basketball system suffers when kids make a charade of going to college and a coach and school add to the sham. . . .[81]

Knight believes that a minor-league basketball system would not only help to clean up college basketball but would also benefit the NBA by helping to develop the talent of athletes who declare for the draft straight out of high school. Currently, teams must draft based on potential rather than current ability, and therefore allow seventeen- and eighteen-year-old draftees with great promise to sit on the bench while collecting huge paychecks. Knight's proposal differs from Telander's in that the minor-league teams would not be sponsored by universities. However, Knight believes college basketball could continue to prosper. He writes: "The college game has something worthwhile to sell, too: the opportunity to earn a college degree. People who snicker at that don't belong in college basketball. If we don't believe that's a primary objective, why should a kid?"[82]

- **Should football and basketball sponsor minor leagues, like baseball and hockey do? Would anyone watch?**

Some people who call for compensation of college athletes realize that resistance to paying college athletes remains widespread and therefore propose alternative sources of revenue. In a law review article, David Netzley proposes a system that would sidestep the controversial issue of schools paying athletes; instead, he would allow athletes to directly negotiate endorsement deals with advertisers such as shoe companies. He believes that paying college athletes poses too many legal problems: In addition to the probability that athletes would become eligible for expensive workers' compensation coverage, they could unionize to demand higher wages. Netzley believes that his proposal would be the best of both worlds: Student-athletes could get a fair share of the money in college sports, while universities would not be placed in the disadvantageous position of being their athletes' employers.

Netzley criticizes as hypocrisy the NCAA's principle that "student athletes should be protected from exploitation by professional and commercial enterprises," writing that the NCAA itself engages in such exploitation of young athletes:

> [B]owl-game patches worn by athletes may include the name or logo of the corporate sponsor. . . . [The] NCAA can in effect put the athletes on the table and watch corporate sponsors engage in a bidding war. . . . [The NCAA] has seemingly established a monopoly allowing it to take advantage of student-athletes for purposes of generating revenue.[83]

The fair solution, Netzley believes, is to allow the athletes themselves to strike the endorsement deals. College athletes could make a decent amount of money that way, eliminating the perceived unfairness of everyone else capitalizing on their academic success: "[C]ollegiate products are an enormous source of revenue for a variety of commercial enterprises, and this is mainly due to the popularity of certain athletes. In other words, certain amateur athletes are just as marketable, if not more, as their professional equivalent depending on the market."[84] While top college athletes with a national profile might strike deals with shoe companies under Netzley's plan, college athletes in states with no major professional sports franchises but extremely popular college sports teams could strike regional deals. For example, a Nebraska football player might do television commercials for a car dealership, or an Iowa basketball player might do a commercial for a local grocery chain.

Under Netzley's system, of course, not every athlete would receive compensation through endorsement deals. However, his proposal sidesteps a key point of criticism of paying college athletes—that it is unfair to compensate athletes in revenue-generating sports such as football and men's basketball while ignoring hardworking athletes in sports such as wrestling, swimming, and track. Netzley would leave the compensation issue to the free market rather than to university officials: "[A]thletics have from the beginning developed around competition, and thus, it should be the amateur athletes' duty to promote their sport, as well as improve their athletic skills."[85] He believes that some of the top athletes in nonrevenue sports might be able to strike deals with manufacturers of equipment, such as a swimming champion endorsing a particular brand of swimsuit.

> • **Is it fair to say that athletes cannot do advertisements, even if the school does not pay them?**

Although proposals such as those made by Sack and Staurowsky, Telander, Knight, and Netzley differ in the details, they share a common trait: They all acknowledge that not all young athletes are the same. Some play college sports because they love to compete and want an education. Other so-called student-athletes view college sports as an entry-level job in the lucrative field of professional sports. What each of these proposals calls for is that the former type of athlete should be able to compete in a more pure form of amateur athletics, while those in the "big time" deserve some sort of compensation other than a college education, which they might not value highly.

Current NCAA regulations prohibit any payments to athletes, or any other types of benefits, other than the expenses of a college education. Critics of these rules say that requiring athletes to take a "vow of poverty" makes them resentful and vulnerable to corruption by gamblers. They say that college athletes should be paid because they work hard and because so many other people profit from college sports. A few people have gone so far as to suggest that big-time college sports teams should feature professionals who do not actually have to attend the school.

Student-Athletes Should Not Be Allowed to Profit From College Sports

At the end of the 1998 football season, the University of Wisconsin football team electrified its fans by earning a spot in the Rose Bowl, long the ultimate goal of football teams in the Big Ten conference. In addition to glory, participation in the Rose Bowl earned the university's athletic department a $1.8 million check. Payments like this are the ammunition of people who call for paying college athletes; however, the team spent more than $2 million on the game, leaving nothing left over, even if the university had wanted to pay the athletes.

According to professor Murray Sperber, in his book *Beer and Circus,* the athletic department flew a "gravy plane" to the bowl game in southern California, including coaches' families (not to mention baby-sitters), athletic department employees and spouses, board of regents members and their spouses, university administrators and spouses, and boosters—832 people in all. In addition to transportation costs, the department spent lavishly on hotels and meals. Sperber quotes a corporate travel manager, who believed the university might have spent one-fifth as much and still traveled quite comfortably, as saying, "These athletic department administrators could give lessons to drunken sailors on how to throw money around."[86]

- **Should universities have rules for how athletic departments spend money?**

The central point of Sperber's book is a belief shared by many: College sports have spun out of control. He and others believe that paying athletes would only worsen the problem and further diminish the integrity of college sports. Critics believe that paying college athletes not only would do nothing to reduce problems of gambling, but would further erode educational opportunities for serious students. Ultimately, other students and the taxpayers are left paying the bill for big-time college sports, and many people would like to see college sports return to true amateurism rather than continue their transformation into professional sports leagues.

Paying student-athletes would not eliminate opportunities for cheating.

Supporters of true amateurism in college athletics reject the idea that paying student-athletes will do anything to resolve the gambling problem. They argue that proponents of paying players use the gambling prevention rationale as an excuse unsupported by facts. Many believe that the problem of gambling is simply too widespread in college sports to deal with the problem indirectly. Sportswriter Gary D'Amato writes:

> Some people think that paying college athletes would remove the temptation. Wrong. The bookies and mobsters and assorted other scum will always be on the periphery. In a lot of ways, fighting problems in NCAA Division I sports is a lot

like fighting the drug problem in America. We can win battles here and there, but we won't win the war until society undergoes some radical changes.[87]

Most proposals for paying student-athletes call for paying them a relatively modest sum, and it is questionable whether a small monthly stipend would really prevent a dishonest athlete from seeking a handsome payoff from a gambler. The fact that a number of professional athletes have been involved in gambling, drug dealing, and other illegal activities demonstrates that even people who make a very comfortable living are not immune to greed for illegal income. In the *Little Rock Free Press*, Robert T. Shields writes: "To pay a player as an incentive to stop gambling misses the point. Gambling erodes the intent and foundation of sports, yet it occurs at almost every level of play. The NCAA paying a player will not stop gambling."[88]

> • **Is a person with no money less likely to gamble than a person with a little bit of money?**

The NCAA, which vehemently opposes paying student-athletes, believes that the only way to deal with the gambling problem is to deal with it head-on, with swift and serious punishment for any athletes found to be involved in gambling. The NCAA also conducts the "Don't Bet on It" campaign, an intensive educational program to educate incoming student-athletes about the moral and legal problems associated with gambling before they get involved in it.

Many critics believe that even if paying players would help to curb gambling, the moral price is simply too high. Paying players to eliminate gambling, it is suggested, would be attacking one vice—gambling—while sacrificing the important virtues of competition and education. An editorial carried by Georgetown University's newspaper labeled the idea of paying college athletes to curb gambling "ridiculous": "[C]ollege athletics isn't supposed to be about money, it's supposed to be about an education, both in academics and athletics. If players were to start getting paid, you can forget [about academics]. . . . If you love college athletics, the idea of paying players has to turn your stomach."[89]

The NCAA agrees. In explaining its opposition to gambling, both legal and illegal, the organization states:

> Sports wagering demeans the value of competition and competitors alike by [sending] a message that is contrary to the purposes and meaning of "sport." Sports competition should be appreciated for the inherent benefits related to participation of student-athletes, coaches, and institutions in fair contests, not the amount of money wagered on the outcome of the competition.[90]

Paying student-athletes would create too many legal problems.

To pay student-athletes would effectively make them employees and thus create many legal complications for universities. Although it might seem like a minor expense to offer athletes a small amount of money, say $150 a month, for participating in sports, this payment would trigger many other expenses and legal obligations for universities, which would raise the cost of sponsoring college athletics so high that many universities might prefer to fold their programs rather than pay the additional costs.

One key cost associated with paying athletes, and thereby making them employees, is the university's responsibility for workers' compensation coverage. Workers' compensation provides monetary compensation to people who are disabled on the job, covering both medical expenses and cash payments to people who cannot work as a result of their injuries. Although courts have held numerous times that athletes are not employees eligible for workers' compensation, the courts' reasoning has relied on the nature of the legal relationship between the universities and athletes, which, in the absence of payment, is harder to construe as an employment relationship. Peter Goplerud writes: "[C]ollegiate sports is big business. If additional money is paid to players it is likely that schools will attempt to exercise more control over them. This is one of the factors used in determining the presence of an employment relationship. At that point, the college scholarship would begin to look more like a professional sports contract. . . ."[91] If they became responsible for workers' compensation coverage, universities might incur especially high costs for covering football players, who risk serious injury on both the practice field and the playing field.

Although most proposals for paying college athletes call for limiting the stipends to a small monthly amount or for awarding the stipends only to players in revenue-generating sports, some legal experts believe it would be difficult to keep the stipends at a low level because of labor laws. Under federal laws, employees have the right to form labor unions, and it is believed that if college athletes were paid, courts would hold that they, too, have the right to unionize. Professional athletes in the major sports leagues are represented by labor unions and therefore can bargain collectively for higher pay and better benefits, and if their demands are not met, the labor union may call for a strike, or work stoppage. In recent years, the NFL, NHL, and Major League Baseball have all had labor-related work stoppages. If college athletes unionized, they might call for a strike as well, write Thomas Hurst and Grier Pressly: "Imagine the bargaining leverage that would arise out of a threat by a highly ranked football team to strike during a contest with an equally ranked opponent."[92] Quickly, the athletes' "laundry money" could become lucrative paychecks that universities simply cannot afford to pay.

> • **Are college athletes likely to go on strike before a big game?**

A number of other legal issues cloud the question of paying student-athletes. For example, courts have held that college athletics are not covered by antitrust laws, which limit "restraints on trade." An example of an illegal restraint on trade is "price-fixing," such as car manufacturers working together to establish maximum prices that they pay for steel to build their products. Courts have generally held that NCAA regulations—which certainly restrain the operation of college athletic departments—are not prohibited restraints of trade because they are designed to help competition. However, a rule limiting the cash compensation of college athletes, Hurst and Pressly believe, might not survive a court's scrutiny because the rule might constitute prohibited price-fixing. Additionally, paying athletes makes collegiate athletics seem even more like a business rather than an educational function, and therefore athletic programs might lose their exemptions from having to pay taxes on their revenues. Another potential pitfall is that paying only those athletes in revenue-generating sports like football would mean that more male athletes than female athletes would be getting paid, a potential violation of federal antidiscrimination laws.

Demanding a fair share for student-athletes ignores the wasteful spending of college athletics.

One of the main arguments in favor of paying college athletes, particularly football and men's basketball players, is that because the sports generate so much money, it is unfair to deny student-athletes a fair share of that money. However, some opponents of paying student-athletes say that this argument misses the point. Because, they say, so many athletic programs actually lose money rather than making a profit, there is really no "share" to go to the athletes, fair or otherwise. Indiana University professor Murray Sperber writes:

> [J]ournalists . . . have logic and ethics on their side when they demand that the athletes receive their fair "share" of the TV pay outs—except, after the athletic directors, coaches, and athletic department staff spend the revenue, nothing remains for the players. Before the athletes can obtain their share, the entire athletic department finance system must be overhauled.[93]

Sperber charges that, as a result of uncontrolled spending, such as that by the University of Wisconsin athletic department during the 1999 Rose Bowl, there is no money left in the pot for the athletes. Even football and men's basketball programs, despite the revenue generated by television, ticket sales, endorsement deals, and merchandise, end up losing money, and frequently the university must spend money from its general educational fund to make up the difference. Adding the expense of paying student-athletes, therefore, would drain even more revenue from the university's educational mission, and other students would suffer.

Additionally, college athletic programs receive many tax breaks from the federal government; because the programs do not pay taxes, it is argued, everyone else must pay higher taxes to make up the difference. As a result, any "pot of money" in college sports comes at least in part from taxpayers—every business and all individuals who pay taxes, whether or not they are sports fans. To say that student-athletes deserve a share of the money in college sports is to say that taxpayers should be partially responsible for the student-athlete's paycheck.

- **Should college sports get tax breaks that professional sports do not get?**

College athletic departments avoid several types of taxes, representing untold millions of dollars for which other taxpayers pick up the tab. One tax from which athletic programs are exempt is the unrelated business income tax (UBIT), which most nonprofit organizations must pay on their revenue-generating activities. Economist Andrew Zimbalist explains that this tax is designed to prevent nonprofit organizations from having an unfair edge over businesses: "[Without the UBIT] a hotel run by a college could charge lower room fees than a private hotel down the street or a college-run bookstore could sell books at lower prices than a private bookstore in town."[94]

Because the NCAA and its member universities are nonprofit

organizations and because selling television rights and corporate sponsorships is a revenue-producing activity, it seems logical that the NCAA and universities would have to pay the UBIT on their lucrative television deals. However, the Internal Revenue Service (IRS), which collects federal taxes, has held that the UBIT does not apply to television deals for college sports. Thus, the hundreds

The IRS Does Not Tax Broadcasting Revenue

An exempt collegiate athletic conference conducts an annual competitive athletic game between its conference champion and another collegiate team. Income is derived from admission charges and the sale of exclusive broadcasting rights to a national radio and television network. An athletic program is considered an integral part of the educational process of a university.

The educational purposes served by intercollegiate athletics are identical whether conducted directly by individual universities or by their regional athletic conference. Also, the educational purposes served by exhibiting a game before an audience that is physically present and exhibiting the game on television or radio before a much larger audience are substantially similar. Therefore, the sale of the broadcasting rights contributes importantly to the accomplishment of the organization's exempt purpose and is not an unrelated trade or business.

In a similar situation, an exempt organization was created as a national governing body for amateur athletes to foster interest in amateur sports and to encourage widespread public participation. The organization receives income each year from the sale of exclusive broadcasting rights to an independent producer, who contracts with a commercial network to broadcast many of the athletic events sponsored, supervised, and regulated by the organization.

The broadcasting of these events promotes the various amateur sports, fosters widespread public interest in the benefits of the organization's nationwide amateur program, and encourages public participation. The sale of the rights and the broadcasting of the events contribute importantly to the organization's exempt purpose. Therefore, the sale of the exclusive broadcasting rights is not an unrelated trade or business.

Source: Internal Revenue Service Pub. No. 598, "Tax on Unrelated Business Income of Exempt Organizations" (March 2000).

of millions of dollars that the NCAA and universities receive each year are not taxed. Critics wonder why college athletes should receive a share of this money, when the government does not, leaving taxpayers with a higher tax bill each year.

College athletic programs also benefit indirectly from a tax benefit given to their boosters. Athletic departments frequently use a two-step method of ticket sales: A person who wishes to buy tickets must contribute a lump sum each year to the athletic program, which then allows the person to purchase tickets to games at face value. Under IRS regulations, a booster whose contribution to a college athletic program allows him or her to purchase tickets to sporting events may deduct (pay no taxes on) 80 percent of the contribution. Zimbalist criticizes this deduction, saying it costs taxpayers tens of millions of dollars annually. He writes: "Sports fans might note a similarity between such booster donations in colleges sports and Personal Seat Licences (PSLs) in professional sports. . . . It is rather like paying to see the menu in a restaurant, then paying for the meal. . . . [A significant] difference is that when one buys a PSL for an NFL team it is not tax-deductible."[95]

Donations to College Athletic Programs Are 80 Percent Deductible

If you make a payment to, or for the benefit of, a college or university and, as a result, you receive the right to buy tickets to an athletic event in the athletic stadium of the college or university, you can deduct 80 percent of the payment as a charitable contribution.

If any part of your payment is for tickets (rather than the right to buy tickets), that part is not deductible. In that case, subtract the price of the tickets from your payment. Eighty percent of the remaining amount is a charitable contribution.

Source: Internal Revenue Service Pub. No. 526, "Charitable Contributions" (December 2000).

Critics such as Murray Sperber and Andrew Zimbalist deny the existence of "pot of money" from which athletes should take their fair share. The fact remains that many college athletic programs lose money, despite television deals, ticket sales, sponsorships, merchandise, bowl games, and tournaments. The big-time spending of big-time college sports not only ends up hurting the universities' educational mission, but it also comes at the expense of taxpayers. Before a fair share can be discussed, universities and the NCAA must change the way that they spend money.

A college education is ample reward for participation in athletics.

Although many people give economic reasons for not paying college athletes, others put their opposition in more idealistic terms. Some believe that the dream of amateurism is too precious to sacrifice, while others believe that all college students benefit from having members of their student body compete against other universities. For example, students at Harvard and Yale are proud of their universities' academic standards, but nothing gets their blood pumping like the annual Harvard-Yale football game.

Some observers, such as professors Sack and Staurowsky, call for a return of "true amateurism" to most universities. They argue in their book *College Athletes for Hire* that not only should most college athletes *not* get paid, but that they should receive financial aid based on financial need rather than on athletic ability. Under their proposed system, the star quarterback from an upper-middle-class background might receive no scholarship assistance, whereas the backup kicker from a low-income family might have his tuition, room and board, and fees paid by the university. Both students would participate in football not for the financial rewards, but for the love of the game. In order to achieve this laudable goal, they write, some universities that have become too tied up in the "arms race" of uncontrolled spending on big-time athletics would have to leave the ranks of college competition and sponsor semiprofessional teams instead.

Although many people are cynical about the idea that college sports would be as exciting if they limited participation to "true" student-athletes who received no scholarships and met strict university academic standards, a few outspoken idealists remain. In his book *The Last Amateurs*, John Feinstein follows the basketball season of the Patriot League, whose member schools, such as Holy Cross and Colgate, follow the Ivy League's model of awarding scholarships solely on the basis of financial need rather than athletic skill. He writes that the Patriot League's games are still exciting, but that the league does not experience the problems of fraud and academic failure experienced by other Division I schools: "The seventeen members of the Class of 2000 in the Patriot League came from diverse backgrounds. . . . Some were far more successful as college basketball players than others. . . . But they all had one thing in common soon after they finished playing college basketball. They were all college graduates." [96]

- **Is a college education a good reward for someone who does not have the academic skills to do well?**

Other people take a more moderate approach, supporting the current system of allowing schools to award full scholarships to student-athletes, but nothing more. To them, a college education is an ample reward, from a financial standpoint. Criticizing a proposal by Nebraska's governor to pay college football players, sports columnist Mike Lopresti writes:

> It will cost an out-of-state student more the $60,000 to get an education at the University of Nebraska. Most will have to work. Many will graduate in debt, the payments stretching out for years. Even the best and brightest of them. It will cost a football player nothing. While there, he will get the finest medical care the school can offer. The best food. Any tutoring help he requests. [97]

Dismissing criticisms that not every college athlete values

the opportunity for a college education, Lopresti provides a personal perspective:

> I have a son who is a senior in high school. He thought about Duke, and I gagged at the annual price tag of $38,230. He mentioned Michigan, and I went into convulsions at $29,508 a year. Had he been a coveted quarterback, he could attend either for free. I wouldn't have felt very exploited. [98]

Sports columnist Jason Whitlock agrees. The former college football player writes:

> [C]ollege athletes are not getting ripped off. Now, they might be allowing themselves to get exploited by not taking advantage of their educational opportunity. But that's within their control. Do you know what people around the world would be willing to endure for a chance to be educated at one of our institutions of higher learning? [People] are dying on makeshift boats . . . every day just trying to sneak over here and live in one of our "slums." And I'm supposed to feel sorry because a university is selling a jersey and not kicking back a few of the dollars to Joe Running Back? [99]

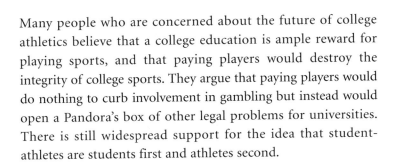

Many people who are concerned about the future of college athletics believe that a college education is ample reward for playing sports, and that paying players would destroy the integrity of college sports. They argue that paying players would do nothing to curb involvement in gambling but instead would open a Pandora's box of other legal problems for universities. There is still widespread support for the idea that student-athletes are students first and athletes second.

Requiring Equality Between Men's and Women's Athletics Is Impractical

In the state of Wisconsin, wrestling is a popular sport among high school boys. However, it is becoming more difficult for wrestlers to continue to compete at the college level without going to school out of state. In 2001, Marquette University, located in Milwaukee, disbanded its wrestling team, leaving only two Wisconsin universities with wrestling teams. According to the *Milwaukee Journal-Sentinel*, the reasons for eliminating the team were not financial; in fact, the university had stopped funding the team in the 1990s, but "the program survived another seven years without a dime from the school because of loyal alumni who raised scholarship money themselves. The coach made more money at his second job as a personal trainer."[100]

The continuation of the wrestling team seemed like a win-win situation for the university. The school was able to recruit people interested in wrestling without spending any funds, and the scholarships created by the alumni actually provided tuition money to the university. The school's athletic director, Bill Cords, told the newspaper that the team was eliminated because it was not competitive: It had only two winning seasons in eleven years. However, the underlying reason for getting rid of the team was that the university simply had too many male athletes and too few female athletes, and eliminating the wrestling team was an easy way to "even things out."

Why did the university do this? The answer lies both in NCAA policies and in federal law. When Congress passed Title IX of the Education Amendments of 1972, very few women were able to participate in college athletics, since schools simply did not offer women's sports teams, provided grossly inadequate funding, or had teams only in traditionally "female" sports such as gymnastics and equestrian events. Congress acted in this landmark legislation to end discrimination against women's sports and provide equal opportunities for male and female athletes. However, people differ in their opinions of what "equal opportunity" means. As interpreted by the federal government, the law requires each university either to have a percentage of female athletes equal to the percentage of female students in the student body or to show in other ways that the university is accommodating female student-athletes, such as by adding women's sports teams on a regular basis or creating sports teams in which female students have expressed interest.

For Marquette, adding women's sports teams was not an option. The wrestling team had originally lost its funding due to the university's financial problems, and the costs of establishing new women's sports teams made such a move impractical. So, instead, the university limited the number of roster spots on its men's teams. When that was not enough to bring the number of athletes of each gender into balance, the school ultimately dropped the wrestling program. With the help of the National

Wrestling Coaches Association, the Marquette wrestlers sued the federal government, charging that Title IX is a form of "reverse discrimination." Although the lawsuit was unsuccessful at the trial level, opponents of Title IX continue their fight in courts and in Congress.

> • Is there a difference between eliminating a team and not starting one in the first place? Which group of athletes is worse off?

Title IX imposes a quota on male and female athletes.

Very few people disagree with the basic premise of Title IX—that educational institutions should not discriminate against women. However, many people disagree with the way that Title IX is enforced, saying that it is unfair to impose quotas, or manipulate the number of male and female athletes who are allowed to participate in intercollegiate sports. Universities frequently make decisions based on the first part of a three-part test developed by the U.S. Department of Education: whether the percentage of female athletes coincides with the number of female students. In other words, if 55 percent of a university's students are women, then approximately 55 percent of its athletes should be women, according to the standard.

In general, the law disfavors numerical quotas when it comes to the enforcement of civil rights laws. For example, the U.S. Supreme Court has recently reaffirmed that universities may not legally use numerical quotas in their affirmative action policies, meaning that schools may not reserve a certain number of spots in their classes for African Americans, Hispanics, and Native Americans. However, the Department of Education's Office for Civil Rights continues to maintain that universities may set aside a certain number of athletic opportunities for women.

Athletic participation under Title IX

A Bush administration commission is considering relaxing the standards set by a 1972 statute, called Title IX, that prohibits gender discrimination in education programs receiving federal funds.

The statute is largely credited with enabling the increasing participation of women and girls in collegiate and high school athletics.

High school participation

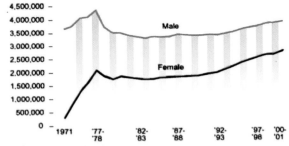

Collegiate participation

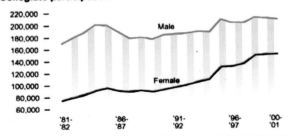

SOURCES: National Federation of State High School Associations; Women's Sports Foundation; National Collegiate Athletic Association   AP

Some critics argue that Title IX has not succeeded in bringing gender equality to college athletics. Others point to a trend of increasing numbers of young women taking part in sports. These charts, produced in 2003, compare high school and college sports participation (by gender), indicating a consistent upward trend for females and a more or less steady figure for males. Overall, female participation in school athletics has greatly increased since Title IX's gender equality laws went into effect in 1972.

Department of Education's Legal Test for Title IX Compliance

[The Department of Education's Office for Civil Rights (OCR)] will apply the following three-part test to assess whether an institution is providing nondiscriminatory participation opportunities for individuals of both sexes:

1. Whether intercollegiate level participation opportunities for male and female students are provided in numbers substantially proportionate to their respective enrollments; or

2. Where the members of one sex have been and are underrepresented among intercollegiate athletes, whether the institution can show a history and continuing practice of program expansion which is demonstrably responsive to the developing interests and abilities of the members of that sex; or

3. Where the members of one sex are underrepresented among intercollegiate athletes, and the institution cannot show a history and continuing practice of program expansion, as described above, whether it can be demonstrated that the interests and abilities of the members of that sex have been fully and effectively accommodated by the present program....

Thus, the three-part test furnishes an institution with three individual avenues to choose from when determining how it will provide individuals of each sex with nondiscriminatory opportunities to participate in intercollegiate athletics. If an institution has met any part of the three-part test, OCR will determine that the institution is meeting this requirement....

OCR will consider the following factors, among others, as evidence that may indicate a history of program expansion that is demonstrably responsive to the developing interests and abilities of the underrepresented sex:

- an institution's record of adding intercollegiate teams, or upgrading teams to intercollegiate status, for the underrepresented sex;

- an institution's record of increasing the numbers of participants in intercollegiate athletics who are members of the underrepresented sex; and

- an institution's affirmative responses to requests by students or others for addition or elevation of sports.

OCR will consider the following factors, among others, as evidence that may indicate a continuing practice of program expansion that is demonstrably responsive to the developing interests and abilities of the underrepresented sex:

- an institution's current implementation of a nondiscriminatory policy or procedure for requesting the addition of sports (including the elevation of club or intramural teams) and the effective communication of the policy or procedure to students; and

- an institution's current implementation of a plan of program expansion that is responsive to developing interests and abilities....

OCR will determine whether there is sufficient unmet interest among the institution's students who are members of the underrepresented sex to sustain an intercollegiate team. OCR will look for interest by the underrepresented sex as expressed through the following indicators, among others:

- requests by students and admitted students that a particular sport be added;

- requests that an existing club sport be elevated to intercollegiate team status;

- participation in particular club or intramural sports;

- interviews with students, admitted students, coaches, administrators, and others regarding interest in particular sports;

- results of questionnaires of students and admitted students regarding interests in particular sports; and

- participation in particular in interscholastic sports by admitted students.

In addition, OCR will look at participation rates in sports in high schools, amateur athletic associations, and community sports leagues that operate in areas from which the institution draws its students in order to ascertain likely interest and ability of its students and admitted students in particular sport(s)....

OCR will determine whether there is sufficient ability among interested students of the underrepresented sex to sustain an intercollegiate team. OCR will examine indications of ability such as:

- the athletic experience and accomplishments—in interscholastic, club, or intramural competition—of students and admitted students interested in playing the sport;

- opinions of coaches, administrators, and athletes at the institution regarding whether interested students and admitted students have the potential to sustain a varsity team; and

- if the team has previously competed at the club or intramural level, whether the competitive experience of the team indicates that it has the potential to sustain an intercollegiate team.

Neither a poor competitive record nor the inability of interested students or admitted students to play at the same level of competition engaged in by the institution's other athletes is conclusive evidence of lack of ability. It is sufficient that interested students and admitted students have the potential to sustain an intercollegiate team....

Source: U.S. Department of Education, Office for Civil Rights, "Clarification of Intercollegiate Athletics Policy Guidance: The Three-Part Test" (January 16, 1996).

Supporters of Title IX deny that the law operates as a quota system because universities can comply with Title IX by meeting one of the other two parts of the department's three-part test. A university may adhere to part two by demonstrating a "history and continuing practice of program expansion" of women's sports, and may comply with part three by showing "that the interests and abilities of [women] have been fully and effectively accommodated by the present program."[101] In other words, even if a university with a student body that is 55 percent female does not have a 55 percent female athletic program, the university can avoid legal problems if it shows that it has been adding women's sports teams or that it has responded to requests from female students to develop athletic teams for women.

In practice, however, the test operates as a quota system because serious doubt can be cast upon a university's compliance with either of the other two parts of the test by showing that women are underrepresented in the athletic program. Essentially, critics charge, Title IX boils down to a one-part test, and that test is a numerical quota. Carol Zaleski, former USA Swimming president, said, "The unfortunate truth is that Title IX has evolved into something never intended. The act was intended to expand opportunity. The interpretation for the Office for Civil Rights and the evolved enforcement has turned into a quota program. Title IX is a good law with bad interpretation."[102]

- **Are quotas on gender or race fair?**

A recent decision by the University of Northern Iowa (UNI) provides an example of how a university's actions are tied to its percentage of female athletes. When the university announced a decision to eliminate the swimming and diving teams and tennis teams—for both men and women—a law firm representing female athletes at the university sent a threatening letter to the school. In a letter sent to the president of UNI, Trial Lawyers for Public Justice (TLPJ), wrote:

> [P]rior to eliminating the women's swimming and diving and tennis teams, U.N.I.'s intercollegiate athletic program offered women 36.4 percent of the opportunities to participate, even though female undergraduate enrollment was 58.1 percent. These numbers are clearly disproportionate, so U.N.I. fails the first test for compliance. . . . Furthermore, U.N.I.'s elimination of the women's swimming and diving and tennis teams precludes it from meeting the second and third tests. . . . [The] school does not have a history and continuing practice of program expansion responsive to the developing interests and abilities of women and is not fully and effectively accommodating the interests and abilities of women. For these reasons, we believe that U.N.I. is plainly in violation of Title IX. . . .
>
> We believe that the members of the women's swimming and diving teams, and other women athletes and potential athletes at U.N.I., have legally valid and enforceable claims against the University for violating Title IX. Unless we are able to resolve their claims without the need for litigation, we are prepared to file suit. If we succeed in litigation, U.N.I. will be required to alter its conduct, come into compliance with the myriad requirements of Title IX, and reimburse us for the costs and attorneys' fees we and our co-counsel incurred during the course of the litigation.[103]

Responding to the potential costs of a lawsuit, the university reversed its decision to eliminate the women's teams, but continued with its plans to eliminate the men's swimming and diving team and tennis team. The conflict is obvious: If a university cannot demonstrate proportionality, it can only cut men's teams and can only add women's teams. If a university cannot demonstrate proportionality, its hand are tied when it comes to eliminating unpopular teams such as men's and women's gymnastics, even though getting rid of gymnastics might free up more money in the athletic department's budget to spend on other sports. Similarly, if a university cannot demonstrate proportionality, then it can only add women's teams. For example, if the sport of floorball, similar to hockey and wildly popular in Europe, suddenly became widely played in the United States, universities would be required to add women's floorball teams but not men's teams.

> • **Do universities have the freedom to gauge women athletes' interest, or do they have to stick to the numbers?**

Perhaps the best evidence that Title IX has resulted in a quota system is the frequency with which supporters of women's athletics use evidence of unequal numbers of male and female athletes to claim that the federal government is not enforcing the law. For example, the executive director of the Women's Sports Foundation writes: "[M]ales comprise . . . 58% of college athletic participants, receive 64% of athletic operating budgets and $133 million more in college athletic scholarships each year."[104] Despite the rhetoric that schools have other ways of complying with Title IX, many advocates will not rest until female athletes outnumber men and funding for women's athletics exceeds that for men's athletics.

Eliminating men's teams to create women's teams harms innocent and dedicated athletes.

Some of the most vocal critics of Title IX have been wrestling coaches and coaches in other men's sports that do not generate revenue, such as gymnastics, golf, track and field, and baseball. In the past two decades, universities have eliminated dozens of teams in each of these sports. Critics blame these cuts on Title IX, saying that universities drop men's teams in order to meet Title IX's proportionality requirement. Although the law does not strictly require proportionality, experience—such as the circumstances at UNI—shows that lawsuits are successful in pressuring universities to take measures that bring them closer to the proportionality standard.

Title IX's proportionality criterion imposes no minimum standards for the total number of athletic opportunities. It simply requires the percentages of male and female athletes to mirror the percentages of male and female students at the university. Under Title IX, it would be better for a university with 10,000 male students and 10,000 female students to have 15 male athletes and 15 female athletes than to have 315 male athletes and 215 female athletes. The unfortunate reality for many young men participating in less popular sports is that it is much easier for universities to eliminate male athletes than it is for schools to add female athletes.

- **Does eliminating opportunities for men do anything to help women if women's teams are not added?**

Commission on Opportunity in Athletics Criticizes Eliminating Men's Teams

The loss of teams … eloquently described by many of the people affected … have caused the Commission great concern. Although the Commission recognizes that the decision to drop a team is affected by many factors, it should be made clear to schools that it is not a favored way of complying with Title IX. The fundamental premise of Title IX is that decisions to limit opportunities should not be made on the basis of gender. Therefore, educational institutions should pursue all other alternatives before cutting or capping any team when Title IX compliance is a factor in that decision.

Source: Secretary of Education's Commission on Opportunity in Athletics, "'Open to All': Title IX at Thirty" (February 28, 2003).

According to testimony given to a congressional committee by wrestling coach T. J. Kerr, these cuts harm male athletes in two ways: Universities either eliminate entire men's sports programs, or they limit the number of male athletes who may participate on existing teams. Limits on the number of male athletes on a team are particularly likely to affect "walk-ons," or people who have not received athletic scholarships. According to Kerr's testimony:

> Both of these approaches to achieving "gender equity" are wrong. Programs should not be eliminated because athletes matriculate at a school in the good faith belief that the administration will honor its commitment to provide a program for their four years of college. . . .

Commission on Opportunity in Athletics Criticizes Capping Walk-ons

A number of witnesses have told Commissioners that male athletes currently walk-on to teams at greater levels than do females. It has been alleged that this has led institutions to limit the number of men allowed to walk-on to teams, a practice known as roster management. Roster management may control the appearance of disproportional representation, but it does not create any corresponding benefit for the sex not subject to roster management. . . .

[E]ven if the interest of men and women in taking advantage of walk-on opportunities is not the same, no one should be discouraged from walking on to teams for artificial reasons. . . . Limiting walk-ons for reasons other than those related to lack of institutional resources or coaching decisions has serious ramifications for students who are not allowed to participate in athletics. Schools should not impose these kinds of artificial barriers to such participation.

Source: Secretary of Education's Commission on Opportunity in Athletics, "'Open to All': Title IX at Thirty" (February 28, 2003).

The capping of male sports is equally discriminatory and destructive. In this circumstance a young man pays tuition, walks onto a team, works as hard as a first-teamer, but simply does not have the skills to compete at the highest levels [and earn one of the school's limited number of scholarships]. . . . The school dumps them because they are the most expendable.[105]

Many coaches and other critics of Title IX are especially opposed to capping rosters because allowing walk-on athletes to participate costs the university nothing, and an unlimited number of women, if they were interested, have the option to walk-on to women's sports teams. And in the case of Marquette University's wrestling team, the school eliminated an entire team that cost the university nothing, simply because male athletes outnumbered women.

Women are less interested in sports than men are.

Cuts to men's athletics are coming despite large increases in athletic opportunities for women. According to the *Milwaukee Journal-Sentinel*, the overall number of female NCAA athletes more than doubled between 1981 and 2000, growing from fewer than 75,000 to more than 150,000. During the same period, the overall number of male athletes increased by about one-quarter to 210,000. However, more than one-third of the NCAA's 363 wrestling programs were eliminated, leaving only 234 programs.[106]

The wrestling coaches' group and other Title IX opponents bristle at the fact that universities are eliminating opportunities for men to compete even though there might be many additional chances for women to compete on existing teams. Currently, however, the number of unfilled opportunities for female athletes are not relevant to federal enforcement of Title IX. The Department of Education considers only the actual number of participants, not the opportunities available to participate. The *Journal-Sentinel* uses the following example: "[If] only 20 women show up to make [a] 40-woman roster softball team, then in most cases only 20 men would be allowed to play on the baseball team, even if 40 men were interested." [107]

Some experts believe that the newspaper's example is far from theoretical. Attorney Melinda Sidak writes: "[W]omen are not taking advantage of the opportunities already out there. Many college women's teams cannot fill their squads." [108] She compares the average sizes of baseball squads against softball squads, and men's track and field and lacrosse teams against women's teams. According to the NCAA's *1982–2002 Sponsorship and Participation Report*, the average baseball team had 30 men on it, versus 17 women per softball team; the average outdoor track team featured 31 men as opposed to 26 women; and the average for lacrosse teams was 31 men, compared with 21 women. [109]

In sum, universities sponsored 8,151 men's teams and 8,920 women's teams during the 2001–2002 academic year—nearly 10 percent more women's teams than men's teams. However, although more teams were available to female athletes, many more male athletes participated on the teams that were available to them: 212,140 male athletes, compared to 155,513 female athletes.

Part of this difference can be attributed to football. No other sport uses as many players during the course of a game, a fact reflected in the average roster size of ninety-four men. The large number of football players makes it difficult for schools to balance the ratio of male and female athletes. Supporters of Title IX frequently cite the large number of football roster spots as a reason that universities have trouble balancing the number of male and female athletes. Football coaches have vigorously defended maintaining rosters nearly twice the size of NFL rosters, citing playing time lost to injury and the need for younger players to practice before playing in games. Plus, they say, football programs bring in revenue that is used to fund women's sports; it is no coincidence that schools with successful football programs also tend to offer more sports for women. Some people have, therefore, argued that football should actually be exempted from the equation when determining whether a university provides proportional opportunities for men and women.

> • **Should the federal government count the number of spots a university has available on its women's teams or the actual number of athletes?**

Many Title IX opponents wonder whether the difference in the overall *number* of athletes is really that important, given the larger number of women's programs and the number of unfilled *opportunities* for women. They ask: Isn't Title IX about equal *opportunity*? In the words of Katherine Kersten of the Center of the American Experiment, "The proportionality test purports to be a test of gender fairness, but its logic rests on one critical and dubious assumption, that males and females at every college in the nation have an equal desire to play competitive team sports."[110] The primary problem with the federal government's enforcement approach might be that nowhere in the Department of Education's three-part test is the interest in men's sports taken into account. In other words, a university can prove that it is complying with Title IX only if it proves that it is meeting the interests of female students.

Suppose, for example, that on a campus of 25,000 students, 150 men want to play football and 22,000 students want to watch football games on Saturday. At this hypothetical university, a group of four women wants to start an archery team. Under the Department of Education's test, the university would be obligated to fund a new archery team rather than a new football team if funding the new football team would result in there being too many male athletes on campus. To opponents of Title IX, such a legal conclusion is absurd.

> • **Should fan interest play a part in determining the balance between men's and women's sports?**

Very few people would openly deny that women deserve an equal opportunity to participate in college sports, but many believe that women already have equal opportunity, as evidenced by the greater number of women's teams than men's teams. They therefore criticize the use of Title IX, a federal law, to require that schools add female athletes or reduce the number of male athletes. Supporters of nonrevenue sports such as wrestling blame Title IX for a decline in the number of men's teams, and say that women's lesser interest in sports justifies increased spending on men's sports and maintaining higher numbers of male athletes.

Fairness Requires Universities to Spend Equally on Men's and Women's Athletics

E ach year, young women have more and more role models, as women's athletics continue to reach new heights. The recent development of women's professional leagues in basketball and soccer has been possible in large part because of the popularity of these sports at the collegiate level. The women's NCAA basketball tournament has been drawing increasing numbers of spectators and television viewers, and during the twenty-year span from 1982 to 2002, the number of women's collegiate soccer teams skyrocketed from 80 to 868, as the sport has become one of the most popular for girls and young women to play.

The 1999 women's soccer World Cup was a turning point for women's spectator sports. Although women's events in the Olympics had always drawn viewers, people had for years doubted whether women's professional sports could ever become a commercial success. But during the 1999 World Cup, the U.S. women's team sold out the Rose Bowl and Giants Stadium. The final game at the Rose Bowl drew more than ninety thousand fans, with an estimated 40 million television viewers. In the climactic overtime shoot-out, Mia Hamm, the biggest star of the women's game, converted on a penalty kick, setting up teammate Brandi Chastain for a dramatic moment. With the score tied and with China having used all of its penalty kicks, the U.S. team had one final opportunity to win. Chastain's shot past the Chinese goaltender and her subsequent celebration, which made the cover of *Sports Illustrated*, took women's team sports to the next level.

> • **Why did so many more people watch the women's World Cup than usually watch professional women's sports?**

According to late U.S. Representative Patsy Mink, who twenty-seven years earlier had helped pass Title IX, the law guaranteeing equal opportunity for women in college athletics, the victory for women's sports showed how far women athletes had come in those twenty-seven years:

> This victory was significant not only for its impact on women's athletics but as a testament to the power of Congress to change the nation for the better. Mia Hamm, one of the team's brightest stars, was born in 1972—the same year that Title IX was signed into law. Without Title IX, she and many of her teammates may never have had the opportunity to develop their talents and pursue their dreams.[111]

Title IX is not a quota system.

Supporters of women's athletics accuse opponents of Title IX enforcement of misleading the public. Each time a university disbands its wrestling team or men's golf team, critics blame the team's elimination on government-imposed "quotas" on male and female athletes. They say, "The university got rid of our wrestling team because of Title IX. The federal government says that we have to have more female athletes than male athletes." While commemorating Title IX's thirtieth anniversary in 2002, Representative Mink responded:

> This argument is unsupportable. The Department of Education's regulations regarding Title IX do not require schools to cut men's teams in order to comply with Title IX. Rather, "proportionality" is only one of three ways that schools can comply with the law. They may (1) offer athletic opportunities in substantial proportion to male and female enrollment, or (2) show that the institution is steadily increasing opportunities for women students over time, or (3) show that the athletic interests and abilities of female students are being met. Institutions do not need to demonstrate all three.[112]

While acknowledging that Title IX enforcement is based on a three-part test, opponents argue that the test does not truly have three parts because lack of proportionality can be used to prove that a university is not complying with the other two parts of the test. For example, women athletes can point to an imbalance in the number of female athletes as evidence either to show that the university is not expanding women's teams fast enough or to show that the university is not accommodating women's athletic interests. However, supporters of Title IX enforcement deny that proportionality is required. As Assistant Secretary of Education for Civil Rights Norma V. Cantu explains: "The fact that each part of the three-part test considers participation rates does not mean, as some opponents of the test have suggested, that the three parts do not provide different ways to comply with Title IX."[113]

Eliminating men's teams is an acceptable means of creating gender equity.

Supporters of women's athletics maintain that Title IX is unfairly being blamed for decisions to eliminate men's sports teams. The real culprits, they say, are university budgets and wasteful football programs. Universities' decisions to drop less-popular sports such as wrestling teams have more to do with trimming the athletic department budget than with achieving gender proportionality, but Title IX provides a convenient scapegoat. Similarly, universities with football programs must devote extensive resources, and nearly one hundred roster spots, to football. But rather than eliminating football to bring the men's athletic budget in line with the

Court of Appeals Rules That LSU Violated Title IX

[Louisiana State University (LSU) argues] brazenly that the evidence did not demonstrate sufficient interest and ability in fast-pitch softball at LSU and that, therefore, they cannot be liable under Title IX. The heart of this contention is that an institution with no coach, no facilities, no varsity team, no scholarships, and no recruiting in a given sport must have on campus enough national-caliber athletes to field a competitive varsity team in that sport before a court can find sufficient interest and abilities to exist. It should go without saying that adopting this criteria would eliminate an effective accommodation claim by any plaintiff, at any time. In any event, the district court's finding that the requisite level of interest existed is a finding of fact subject to review for clear error. Having reviewed the record, we determine that the district court did not clearly err because there was ample indication of an interest by women in fast-pitch softball....

LSU's hubris in advancing this argument is remarkable, since of course fewer women participate in sports, given the voluminous evidence that LSU has discriminated against women in refusing to offer them comparable athletic opportunities to those it offers its male students.

Source: *Pederson v. Louisiana State University*, 213 F.3d 858 (5th Cir. 2000)

women's athletic budget and the number of male athletes down closer to the number of female athletes, many schools make the conscious decision to keep football and eliminate other men's sports instead.

Is reducing athletic opportunities for men the answer? Although the Commission on Opportunity in Athletics assembled by the Department of Education recommended that the department discourage schools from cutting men's programs or capping walk-on spots, the Department of Education has not yet adopted a policy. Some supporters of women's sports

D.C. Court: Title IX Not to Blame for Loss of Wrestling Programs

[E]ven if the Court granted the relief requested, plaintiffs and their opponents would still be arguing their respective positions to educational institutions, including Bucknell, Marquette, and Yale, which would, in turn, continue to make discretionary determinations with respect to capping, cutting and adding teams based on a number of factors, including those set forth in [Department of Education] Regulations, as well as factors separate and apart from Title IX and its attendant regulations....

Educational institutions selecting athletic offerings exercise discretion within a complex regulatory scheme which requires consideration of a multitude of factors beyond the effective accommodation of the interests and abilities of members of both sexes, the regulatory factor under which the Three Part Test is applied....These include, among others, distribution of facilities, coaching, and scholarship resources among teams, male and female, scheduling of practice time and games, and the competitiveness of various teams....Furthermore, factors external to the regulatory scheme come into play in athletic program decision-making, including the desire to achieve a particular competitive level, availability of athletes with high school competition experience, and spectator interest.

Source: *National Wrestling Coaches Association* v. *U.S. Department of Education*, No. 02-72 (Dist. D.C., June 11, 2003).

believe that, sometimes, limiting opportunities for men is necessary to redress the discrimination that women athletes have faced since the beginning of collegiate competition. Attorney Joanna Grossman writes: "If cutting men's teams were not sometimes an option, then it would be impossible for schools to cure past discrimination without dramatically expanding their budget for athletics, an option not available to most schools."[114]

In Grossman's view, the reason that so many men's teams existed to begin with was that universities discriminated against women's athletics. Had the universities been required to treat men and women equally at the start, then there would never have been so many wrestling teams, baseball teams, and men's golf teams and so few women's teams. She gives the following example: "A school has a men's lacrosse team and a men's hockey team, and no women's teams in either sport. It can't afford new teams, so it cuts men's lacrosse and creates women's hockey. Although the male lacrosse players will be understandably aggrieved . . . the outcome is more fair than the status quo. . . ."[115]

> • **Is it fair to put a person who has worked hard for years at a sport on equal footing with a person who has just developed an interest in a sport?**

Donna Lopiano, executive director of the Women's Sports Foundation, agrees. She testified to the Commission on Opportunity in Athletics:

> It's OK to have sympathy for that walk-on. It's OK to have sympathy for every male who loses his opportunity to play, but you must have unbiased sympathy. You have to feel just as sorry for every woman who didn't have the chance to play, for women who still, at the institutional level, are not getting chances to play, who are not getting benefits, and you simply can't discriminate on the basis of sex in your empathy.[116]

Lopiano and other women's sports advocates believe that the blame for the loss of men's teams in minor sports should be placed not on women's sports, but on football. As she told *Congressional Quarterly Researcher*, she believes that schools should have a proportional number of male and female athletes, and that "men should have the right to pick a sport that has 100 players if they want to use up their opportunities that way." [117] However, when the decision is made to keep football, men must sacrifice other sports teams in order to achieve a proportion of female athletes that represents the percentage of women in the student body.

Referring to her earlier example, in which a school eliminates its men's lacrosse team and adds a women's hockey team, Joanna Grossman writes:

> [W]hen football is the culprit, there is no equality justification for the loss. The men's lacrosse team loses out simply because the brawnier sport wins out. . . . Ideally, men and women should have a team in every sport and if the behemoth of football did not consume such huge resources, that might be possible. But if a new women's team must be created at the expense of an old male team, that is only fair. [118]

Countering arguments that football actually helps schools comply with Title IX by providing revenue that can be used to fund women's teams, Lopiano cites statistics showing that 36 percent of Division I-A and 81 percent of Division I-AA football teams lose money. She writes: "There are no football geese laying golden eggs. There are only fat geese eating the food that could fund additional opportunities for women." [119] Lopiano believes that if a university does not have enough money to sponsor a sufficient number of teams to meet all male and female students' interests, then it must make tough decisions, such as eliminating or not starting teams, in order to ensure that men and women have equal opportunities.

Others agree that universities should not be allowed to make economic justifications for limiting women's sports, given the vast expenditures made on men's sports. In a law review article, Megan Starace writes: "If a university's method of funding athletic programs for one gender is equivalent to the percentage of that gender's membership in the student body, it can be assumed that even if the university is not able to meet the interests of all students, it has divided the athletic funding that it can afford in an even manner."[120] In other words, when times are tough, it is unfair to make women bear the burden more than men. Sportswriter Lori Nickel puts it this way: "If you have a son and a daughter, shouldn't things be equal? Would you buy your boy hockey equipment and then tell your daughter that there's no money left over for her softball pitching lessons?"[121]

- If people are interested in a particular sport, can't they pick a college that offers that sport? Does this impede their education?

Women have had fewer opportunities to participate in sports than men have.

A few decades ago, most parents probably *would* have bought their sons sports equipment even if they could not afford to buy their daughters any. Americans have had a long-standing societal bias against women participating in sports, and it was reflected in relatively low numbers of female athletes at every level in comparison to male athletes. Opponents of Title IX enforcement frequently argue that universities should not be required or encouraged to provide proportional opportunities for men and women because women are not as interested in sports as men are. However, supporters of women's sports question whether women's interest level in sports can be accurately gauged, in part because of the traditional bias against women's sports.

Supporters of women's athletics accuse universities of not doing enough to encourage women's interest in sports and relying on interest surveys as means of justifying their failure to add more women's sports. Actress Geena Davis is talented enough with a bow and arrow to have almost qualified for the U.S. Olympic team, but she only developed her interest in archery nearly two decades after graduating from Boston University. She testified before the Commission on Opportunity in Athletics, "I am here to take you for a short ride in Thelma and Louise's car if you think that it's fair and just to limit a girl's opportunity to play sports based on her response to an interest survey,"[122] making reference to her movie in which the title characters drive their car off a cliff.

The problem, women's sports advocates say, is that interest in sports requires nurturing. For too many years, women have not had enough positive role models or enough opportunities to compete. By contrast, the news media make superstars out of male athletes, and boys have had many more opportunities to play sports, from early childhood, through every level of school, and continuing into the professional ranks. Using Title IX to expand opportunities for women will likely also develop their interest, writes Grossman: "Watching senior women soccer stars triumph, for example, can motivate a freshman high school girl to follow up on her athletic ambitions. If all the seniors had been cheerleaders and homecoming queens, she might have sacrificed the same ambitions to the ever-present urge to fit in."[123]

• **Should universities be responsible for developing women's interest in sports, or is it too late to do so by the time women reach college age?**

Champions of women's athletics believe it is fair to require colleges to have a number of female athletes that reflects the percentage of women in the student body—even if that means eliminating men's sports teams. Athletic departments have only limited resources, and as long as women's sports lag behind men's sports in participation and funding, any necessary cuts should be made to men's sports rather than to women's. It is no excuse to say that women are less interested in sports, because universities have not done enough to generate interest among female students.

The Future of College Athletics

Many people believe that college sports are booming. Multimillion-dollar television contracts, endorsement deals, and ticket sales have helped some schools generate money during tough economic times. At big schools in powerhouse athletic conferences, revenue-generating sports, such as football and men's basketball, and, to a lesser extent, women's basketball, help to support other sports teams, such as baseball, track, and field hockey. The revenue helps provide more athletic opportunities for women than ever before. At some schools, athletic departments even help generate money for libraries and academic departments.

However, at other schools, the picture is not so rosy. Athletic departments—and even the so-called revenue sports of football and men's basketball—actually *lose* money as schools engage in an "arms race" of escalating spending on coaches, training facilities, and stadiums in an effort to attract recruits and remain competitive. The universities are often left covering the losses of the athletic departments, even as academic departments struggle to pay professors and buy needed books and equipment.

- **Are college sports in trouble? Or are critics overreacting?**

Challenges Facing College Athletics
Clearly, underneath the glory of bowl games and championship tournaments, there lies a number of problems for universities, and several problems also plague young athletes. Many of the top athletes are recruited for their sports-related talent even though they are academically unprepared for college. A sizable percentage of these students leave college without a degree, and others take "soft" classes and get preferential treatment from professors; as a result, they do not learn much, despite the fact that they receive a degree. On the other side of the coin, many women athletes struggle to convince universities to fund sports teams and allow them the same opportunities to compete that men have.

Despite the commercial potential of college sports, more and more people are calling for reform. The perspectives are endless. Some want to pay players as a way of keeping them from turning professional early. Others say that people who cannot make the grade should be playing minor-league sports rather than taking up spaces in college classes that should go to more serious students.

Many attacks focus on the virtually unchecked power of college athletic departments to do what they want with the money they make from television contracts and other sources. Unlike professional teams, the millions that college athletic departments take in from television networks and sponsors is not taxed. And, unlike private businesses, the NCAA is not subjected to the rules of fair play set up under the nation's antitrust laws, which prohibit price-fixing. As a result, the NCAA oversees a system in which colleges use untaxable income to run sporting teams of athletes who are not allowed to earn money.

At the same time, university administrators hold up their hands, saying that there is no money for academic departments or even for adding women's sports. An increasing number of people argue that because college sports have become big business, the laws should treat them like any other business. If athletic departments want to keep the tax breaks reserved for nonprofit organizations, then they should be required to use their money for the public good, as charities do. To some, serving the public good would include helping to fund academics and women's athletics, as well as paying the athletes a fair share of the money made through all their hard work.

The Future of College Football

Perhaps the most controversial college sport is football, for several important reasons. First, maintaining a football team is very expensive. The equipment, the practice facilities, the stadium, and the coaching staff are all major expenses; and because the size of the playing squads and coaching staffs are so large, travel expenses are also quite high. Second, because of the size of the teams, football requires a large number of athletic scholarships. Unlike basketball, in which the number of men's scholarships is often balanced by the number of women's basketball scholarships, maintaining a football team usually means that the university will offer many more scholarships to men than to women. This imbalance has led critics to charge that football makes compliance with federal antidiscrimination laws impossible. Supporters of football, however, have said that football is too important to American history and culture, and if keeping football means more scholarships will go to men than to women, then football should be exempted from Title IX, the law that requires schools to offer equal athletic opportunities for men and women.

- **Is football different from other sports? Is there something special about college football?**

In recent years, the development of the Bowl Championship Series (BCS) in college football has created an additional stir. Although the original idea behind the arrangement—which assigns top football teams to play in selected bowl games—was to resolve controversies over ranking by ensuring that the number-one team played the number-two team, the system has generated controversy about how those rankings are determined. Recently, a group of colleges has asked Congress to take action against the BCS. College football has long enjoyed an exemption from federal antitrust laws, which are designed to keep prices low by preventing businesses from conspiring with one another to keep prices high by eliminating competition. In a sense, the BCS prevents schools from selling their services to the highest bidder, and also prevents the organizers of bowl games from signing the teams of their choice.

The reason that the NCAA and the BCS have been exempted from antitrust laws is that they have persuaded lawmakers that their arrangements do not have the effect of stifling competition, but rather of promoting competition. For example, when the NCAA prohibits teams from paying players, the goal is to promote fair competition by putting everyone on a level playing field. Similarly, the BCS claims that its goal is to provide the best possible football matchups.

However, officials at some schools think that the BCS is more about keeping money within football's powerhouse conferences—the Atlantic Coast Conference (ACC), the Big Twelve, the Big East, the Big Ten, the Pacific Ten, and the Southeastern Conference (SEC)—than providing the best football game. Scott Cowen, the president of Tulane University, expressed his frustration to a congressional committee investigating the BCS.

When talking to his university's football team, he cannot try to inspire them to win a national championship, because, he says, the BCS makes this an impossible dream:

> I cannot tell them that, should they have a terrific season and play with all their heart and soul, they will have a realistic chance to play for a national title. I cannot tell them that the reward for the end of a long and successful season could be an appearance in a major bowl game. Because the truth is, when it comes to Division I-A football in a non-BCS school, no matter how well these young men play, no matter what kind of season they have—they will have virtually no realistic access to major bowls or championship play.
>
> So when Tulane had a perfect football season in 1998, we had no practical chance for a major bowl or a championship run despite being one of only two undefeated teams in the country. The other undefeated team was the University of Tennessee, which won the national championship for which we did not get the chance to compete. When Brigham Young University was at 12–0 in 2001, the team went into its 13th game of the season knowing it had no shot at a title or even a major bowl game. It finished the regular season 12–1, still with a better win-loss percentage than eight of the top-10 schools in the BCS rankings that season. Marshall University's football team went 11–2 the past two years, and it also had a better record than eight of the top-10 BCS-ranked teams. But Marshall was unable to compete for a championship or play in a major bowl because Marshall is not a BCS school.[124]

Athletic departments, both big-time and otherwise, are watching with interest to see how this controversy is resolved. If college football is subjected to federal antitrust laws, it could start the fall of college athletics' house of cards, the current system under which athletic departments rake in millions of dollars from television contracts and endorsement deals while having very little accountability.

> • Should powerful schools be allowed to make an agreement that keeps less-powerful schools out of the championship race?

To many, the economic success of college sports is a blessing both for the colleges and for the athletes who are able to earn a free education. But many critics question how much longer college sports can continue to earn millions of dollars while banning salaries for athletes and remaining exempt from income tax and other laws governing businesses. Some people say that college athletics should return to "true amateurism," with student-athletes who work as hard in the classroom as they do on the field, while others say that college sports have become too exciting and popular to dismantle with cumbersome regulations.

Amateur Athletics Versus Economic Reality

1 *2003–2004 NCAA Division I Manual: Constitution, Operating Bylaws, Administrative Bylaws.* Indianapolis: National Collegiate Athletic Association, 2003, p. 5.
2 Amateur Athletic Association, Bylaw 303.2.3 (2003).
3 Allen J. Sack and Ellen J. Staurowsky, *College Athletes for Hire: The Evolution and Legacy of the NCAA's Amateur Myth.* Westport, CT: Praeger Publishers, 1998.
4 Ibid., p. 16.

Point: High-Profile Athletic Programs Benefit Universities

5 Press Release, Oklahoma University, "OU Athletics Department, University Libraries Create Historic Partnership" (April 10, 2002). Available online at *http://soonersports.ocsn.com/genrel/041002aaa.html.*
6 Mike Krzyzewski with Donald T. Phillips, *Leading With the Heart.* New York: Warner Books, 2000, pp. 189–190.
7 Thad Williamson, *More Than a Game: Why North Carolina Basketball Means So Much to So Many.* Cambridge, MA: Economic Affairs Bureau, 2001, p. 239.
8 Statement by Tulane University President Scott S. Cowen (June 10, 2003). Available online at *http://www.feedback.tulane.edu/cowen_0610.html.*
9 Press Release, Florida A&M University Athletics, "Florida A&M Announces Television Pact With Urban Broadcasting" (June 5, 2003). Available online at *http://www.famusports.com.*
10 Ibid.
11 Duke University Athletics Department, "Mission Statement for Intercollegiate Athletics." Available online at *http://goduke.ocsn.com/ot/mission.html.*
12 Williamson, p. 147.
13 Ibid.
14 Congressional Record H8111 (November 13, 2001).

15 Joe Paterno with Bernard Asbell, *Paterno: By the Book.* New York: Random House, 1989, p. 235.
16 Tom Coyne, "Notre Dame Ponders Impact of an Expanded ACC," *collegesports.com* (May 16, 2003). Available online at *http://www.collegesports.com/sports/m-footbl/stories/051603aah.html.*
17 Gilbert M. Gaul and Frank Fitzpatrick, "College Sports: What Was Sacred Is Now up for Sale," *Philadelphia Inquirer* (September 14, 2000).
18 Bob Knight with Bob Hamel, *Knight: My Story.* New York: St. Martin's Press, 2002, p. 258.
19 Ibid.
20 Information supplied by University of Wisconsin-Madison, Division of Intercollegiate Athletics. Available online at *http://www.uwbadgers.com/badger_fund/priority_points/faq.aspx.*
21 Statement by Andy Geiger. Available online at *http://www.ohiostatebuckeyes.ocsn.com/boosters/osu-boosters.html.*
22 Myles Brand, "Academics First: Progress Report." Speech delivered at National Press Club, Washington, D.C. (March 4, 2003). Available online at *http://www.ncaa.org/releases/MylesBrand/20030304npc.html.*
23 Press Release, Tulane University Athletics Department, "Economic Impact of Tulane Athletics Valued at 42 Million Dollars" (May 30, 2003). Available online at *http://tulanegreenwave.ocsn.com/genrel/053003aaa.html.*

Counterpoint: The Commercialization of Athletics Harms Universities

24 Editorial, "Restore Balance at UI," *Iowa Press-Citizen* (August 24, 2002).
25 John Feinstein, *The Last Amateurs: Playing for Glory and Honor in Division I College Basketball.* Boston: Little, Brown and Company, 2000, pp. 24–25.
26 Ibid., p. 25.
27 Murray Sperber, *Onward to Victory: The Crises That Shaped College Sports.* New York: Henry Holt & Co., 1998, p. 506.
28 Allen J. Sack and Ellen J. Staurowsky, *College Athletes for Hire: The Evolution and Legacy of the NCAA's Amateur*

Myth. Westport, CT: Praeger Publishers, 1998, p. 14.

29 Andrew Zimbalist, *Unpaid Professionals: Commercialism and Conflict in Big-Time College Sports.* Princeton, NJ: Princeton University Press, 1999, p. 171.

30 Sperber, p. 507.

31 John R. Gerdy, "College Athletics As Good Business?" *Sports in School: The Future of an Institution,* ed. John R. Gerdy. New York: Teachers College Press, 2000, p. 45.

32 Sperber, p. 508

33 Zimbalist, pp. 168–169.

34 See *http://www.TexasSports.com/mainpages/001_structure/donor_index.html.*

35 Gerdy, p. 45.

36 Daniel L. Fulks, *Revenues and Expenses of Division I and II Intercollegiate Athletic Programs.* Indianapolis: National Collegiate Athletic Association, 2001.

37 Ibid., pp. 14, 16.

Point: College Athletics Provide Opportunities for Students

38 Dick Vitale with Dick Weiss, *Holding Court: Reflections on the Game I Love.* Indianapolis: Masters Press, 1995, p. 172.

39 Ibid., p. 173.

40 "Large Eligibility Differences Noted by Race, Income," *NCAA News* (February 2, 1998).

41 Myles Brand, "Academics First: Progress Report." Speech delivered at National Press Club, Washington, D.C. (March 4, 2003). Available online at *http://www.ncaa.org/releases/MylesBrand/20030304npc.html.*

42 Ibid.

43 Tom Osborne, *Faith in the Game: Lessons on Football, Work, and Life.* New York: Broadway Books, 1999, p. 129.

44 Miles Krzyzewski with Donald T. Phillips, *Leading With the Heart.* New York: Warner Books, 2000, p. 8.

45 See *http://www.suathletics.com/sports/gen/2001/academicinfo.asp.*

46 Andrew Zimbalist, *Unpaid Professionals: Commercialism and Conflict in Big-Time*

College Sports. Princeton, NJ: Princeton University Press, 1991, p. 30.

47 Bob Knight with Bob Hamel, *Knight: My Story.* New York: St. Martin's Press, 2002, p. 304.

48 Joe Paterno with Bernard Asbell, *Paterno: By the Book.* New York: Random House, 1989, p. 19.

49 Zimbalist, p. 41.

50 Ibid., p. 31.

51 See *http://www.ncaa.org/research/prob_of_competing/.*

52 Paterno, p. 18.

53 Osborne, pp. 7–8.

54 Thad Williamson, *More Than a Game: Why North Carolina Basketball Means So Much to So Many.* Cambridge, MA: Economic Affairs Bureau, 2001, p. 152.

Counterpoint: Athletic Programs Exploit Young People, Especially Minorities

55 Bob Knight with Bob Hamel, *Knight: My Story.* New York: St. Martin's Press, 2002, p. 21.

56 See *http://www.ncaa.org/grad_rates/2003/d1/.*

57 Billy Hawkins, *The New Plantation: The Internal Colonization of Black Student Athletes.* Winterville, GA: Sadiki Press, 2001, p. 75.

58 Andrew Zimbalist, *Unpaid Professionals: Commercialism and Conflict in Big-Time College Sports.* Princeton, NJ: Princeton University Press, 1991, p. 203.

59 William C. Rhoden, "At Conference Tournaments, the Colleges Major in Money," *The New York Times* (March 15, 2003).

60 Ibid.

61 John Feinstein, *The Last Amateurs: Playing for Glory and Honor in Division I College Basketball.* Boston: Little, Brown and Company, 2000, p. 23.

62 Ibid.

63 Hawkins, pp. 19–20.

64 Derrick Gregg, "Race in Athletics: Integration or Isolation," *Sports in School: The Future of an Institution,* ed. John R. Gerdy. New York: Teachers College Press, 2000, p. 84.

65 Hawkins, pp. 75–76.

Point: Athletes Deserve a Share of the Money in Big-Time Sports

66 Joe Paterno with Bernard Asbell, *Paterno: By the Book*. New York: Random House, 1989, p. 188.

67 Dick Vitale with Dick Weiss, *Holding Court: Reflections on the Game I Love*. Indianapolis: Masters Press, 1995, pp. 81–82.

68 Congressional Record H2507 (March 31, 2003).

69 Michael E. Cross and Ann G. Vollano, "The Extent and Nature of Gambling Among College Student Athletes." Available online at *http://www.michigan.edu/~mgoblue/compliance/gambling/conclusion.html*.

70 Allen J. Sack and Ellen J. Staurowsky, *College Athletes for Hire: The Evolution and Legacy of the NCAA's Amateur Myth*. Westport, CT: Praeger Publishers, 1998, p. 91.

71 Ibid., p. 90.

72 Ibid.

73 Ibid., p. 92.

74 Vitale, p. 80.

75 Paterno, p. 190.

76 Sack and Staurowsky, p. 92.

77 Ibid., pp. 130–131.

78 Rick Telander, *The Hundred Yard Lie: The Corruption of College Football and What We Can Do to Stop It*. New York: Simon & Schuster, 1989.

79 Ibid., p. 217.

80 Ibid.

81 Bob Knight with Bob Hamel, *Knight: My Story*. New York: St. Martin's Press, 2002, p. 302.

82 Ibid., p. 303.

83 David C. Netzley II, "Endorsements for Student-Athletes: A Novel Approach to a Controversial Idea," *Stetson Law Forum* (Fall 1997). Available online at *http://www.slaw.stetson.edu/lawforum/back/fall97/netzley.htm*.

84 Ibid.

85 Ibid.

Counterpoint: Student-Athletes Should Not Be Allowed to Profit From College Sports

86 Murray Sperber, *Beer and Circus: How Big-Time College Sports Is Crippling Undergraduate Education*. New York: Henry Holt & Co., 2000, p. 223.

87 Gary D'Amato, "Big Changes Are Needed in College Sports," *Milwaukee Journal-Sentinel* (March 13, 1999).

88 Robert T. Shields, "Athletic Scholarships: End the 'Full Ride,'" *Little Rock Free Press* (February 17, 1999).

89 Tim Sullivan, "College Sports Don't Need Las Vegas," *The Hoya* (September 15, 2000).

90 See *http://www.ncaa.org/membership/enforcement/gambling/index.html*.

91 C. Peter Goplerud, "Stipends for College Athletes: A Philosophical Spin on a Controversial Proposal," *Kansas Journal of Law and Public Policy* (Spring 1996). Available online at *http://www.law.ukans.edu/jrnl/goplerud.htm*.

92 Thomas R. Hurst and J. Grier Pressly III, "Payment of Student-Athletes: Legal and Practical Obstacles," *Villanova Sports and Entertainment Law Journal* 7, no. 1 (2000). Available online at *http://www.vls.law.vill.edu/students/orgs/sports/back_issues/volume7/issue1/payment.html*.

93 Sperber, p. 220.

94 Andrew Zimbalist, *Unpaid Professionals: Commercialism and Conflict in Big-Time College Sports*. Princeton, NJ: Princeton University Press, 1991, p. 128.

95 Ibid., p. 130.

96 John Feinstein, *The Last Amateurs: Playing for Glory and Honor in Division I College Basketball*. Boston: Little, Brown and Company, 2000, p. 403.

97 Mike Lopresti, "College Football Athletes Rewarded Enough Without Pay," *USA Today* (February 12, 2003).

98 Ibid.

99 Jason Whitlock, "College Athletes Already Paid in Full" *ESPN.com Page 2* (September 19, 2002). Available online at *http://espn.go.com/page2/s/whitlock/020919.html*.

Point: Requiring Equality Between Men's and Women's Athletics Is Impractical

100 Lori Nickel, "Title IX Proving to Be More Fatal Than Fruitful," *Milwaukee Journal-Sentinel* (November 7, 2001).

101 U.S. Department of Education, Office for Civil Rights, "Clarification of Intercollegiate Athletics Policy Guidance: The Three-Part Test" (January 16, 1996).

102 Secretary of Education's Commission on Opportunity in Athletics, "'Open to All': Title IX at Thirty" (February 28, 2003).

103 Trial Lawyers for Public Justice to Robert Koob, June 24, 2002.

104 Donna Lopiano, "Gender Equity in Sports: Whose Responsibility Is It?" *Issues and Action* (June 14, 2002). Available online at *http://www. womenssportsfoundation.org/ cgi-bin/iowa/issues/rights/article. html?record=149.*

105 T. J. Kerr, Testimony Before House Education Subcommittee on Post-secondary Education, Training, and Life-Long Learning (May 9, 1995), reprinted in *The CQ Researcher* 7, no. 15 (April 18, 1997).

106 Lori Nickel and Nahal Toosi, "Title IX Is Taken to Task," *Milwaukee Journal-Sentinel* (January 17, 2002).

107 Ibid.

108 Melinda Sidak, "Brown University v. Cohen: A Pyrrhic Victory for Feminists." Available online at *http://www.fed-soc.org/ Publications/practicegroupnewsletters/ civilrights/cr010303.htm.*

109 *1982–2002 NCAA Sponsorship and Participation Report*. Indianapolis: National Collegiate Athletic Association, 2003.

110 Secretary of Education's Commission on Opportunity in Athletics, "Open to All."

Counterpoint: Fairness Requires Universities to Spend Equally on Men's and Women's Athletics

111 Congressional Record H4862 (July 17, 2002).

112 Ibid.

113 Norma V. Cantu, cover letter to U.S. Department of Education, Office for Civil Rights, "Clarification of Intercollegiate Athletics Policy Guidance: The Three-Part Test" (January 16, 1996).

114 Joanna Grossman, "On the Thirtieth Anniversary of Title IX, We Need to Preserve, Not Reverse, Its Guarantee of Equity for Women in College Athletics," *Findlaw's Writ* (June 18, 2002). Available online at *http://writ.findlaw.com/ grossman/20020618.html.*

115 Ibid.

116 Secretary of Education's Commission on Opportunity in Athletics, "'Open to All': Title IX at Thirty" (February 28, 2003).

117 Richard L. Wornsop, "The Issues," *The CQ Researcher* 7, no. 15 (April 18, 1997), p. 341.

118 Grossman, "On the Thirtieth Anniversary."

119 Donna Lopiano, "Gender Equity in Sports: Whose Responsibility Is It?" *Issues and Action* (June 14, 2002). Available online at *http://www. womenssportsfoundation.org/ cgi-bin/iowa/issues/rights/article. html?record=149.*

120 Megan Starace, "Reverse Discrimination Under Title IX: Do Men Have a Sporting Chance?" *Villanova Sports and Entertainment Law Journal* 8, no. 1 (2001). Available online at *http://vls.law.villanova. edu/students/orgs/sports/back_issues/ volume8/issue1/sporting.html.*

121 Lori Nickel, "Title IX Proving to Be More Fatal Than Fruitful," *Milwaukee Journal-Sentinel* (November 7, 2001).

122 Secretary of Education's Commission on Opportunity in Athletics, "Open to All."

123 Grossman, "On the Thirtieth Anniversary."

Conclusion: The Future of College Athletics

124 Testimony before U.S. House of Representatives Committee on the Judiciary, "Competition in College Athletic Conferences and Antitrust Aspects of the Bowl Championship Series" (September 4, 2003).

Feinstein, John. *The Last Amateurs: Playing for Glory and Honor in Division I College Basketball.* Little, Brown and Company, 2000.

Gerdy, John R., ed. *Sports in School: The Future of an Institution.* Teachers College Press, 2000.

Hawkins, Billy. *The New Plantation: The Internal Colonization of Black Student Athletes.* Sadiki Press, 2001.

Knight, Bob, with Bob Hamel. *Knight: My Story.* St. Martin's Press, 2002.

Krzyzewski, Mike, with Donald T. Phillips. *Leading With the Heart.* Warner Books, 2000.

Osborne, Tom. *Faith in the Game: Lessons on Football, Work, and Life.* Broadway Books, 1999.

Paterno, Joe, with Bernard Asbell. *Paterno: By the Book.* Random House, 1989.

Sack, Allen L., and Ellen J. Staurowsky. *College Athletes for Hire: The Evolution and Legacy of the NCAA's Amateur Myth.* Praeger Publishers, 1998.

Sperber, Murray. *Beer and Circus: How Big-Time College Sports Is Crippling Undergraduate Education.* Henry Holt & Co., 2000.

———. *Onward to Victory: The Crises That Shaped College Sports.* Henry Holt & Co., 1998.

Telander, Rick. *The Hundred Yard Lie: The Corruption of College Football and What We Can Do to Stop It.* Simon & Schuster, 1989.

Williamson, Thad. *More Than a Game: Why North Carolina Basketball Means So Much to So Many.* Economic Affairs Bureau, 2001.

Zimbalist, Andrew. *Unpaid Professionals: Commercialism and Conflict in Big-Time College Sports.* Princeton University Press, 1999.

Websites
Amateur Athletic Union (AAU)
www.aausports.org

Organization sponsoring athletic competitions for elementary and high school students, as well as adults playing sports as a hobby.

Black Coaches Association

www.bcasports.org

Coalition of African-American coaches at all levels of athletic competition. Online journal with issues related to coaching.

Center for the Study of Sport in Society

www.sportinsociety.org

Academic center at Northeastern University in Boston devoted to studying sociological aspects of sports, including race, gender, and commercialization.

College Sports Council

www.savingsports.org

Organization devoted to protecting men's college sports from cuts based on Title IX's gender equity requirements.

National Collegiate Athletic Association (NCAA)

www.ncaa.org

National organizing body for collegiate athletics. Regular reports on statistics, such as athletic programs' revenues and losses and athletes' gender, test scores, and graduation rates. Online regulations and rulings.

National Women's Law Center

www.nwlc.org

Public interest law firm specializing in women's rights. Offers information about enforcing Title IX's gender equity requirements.

Presidential Coalition for Athletics Reform

coalition.tulane.edu

Coalition of university presidents opposing the influence of the Bowl Championship Series (BCS) and corporate sponsorship on fair competition in college football.

The Sports Ethics Institute

www.sportsethicsinstitute.org

Links to articles on a wide variety of ethical issues in sports, including amateurism and gender discrimination.

Women's Sports Foundation

www.womenssportsfoundation.org

Organization founded by tennis star Billie Jean King to work for equality for female athletes.

Legislation and Case Law

Principle of Amateurism, NCAA Constitution, Article 2.9
Requires that student-athletes compete for educational purposes and be
protected from commercial exploitation.

Awards, Benefits and Expenses for Enrolled Student-Athletes, NCAA Bylaw 16
Bars NCAA athletes from receiving pay or any benefits beyond the cost of a
college education.

Title IX of the Education Amendments of 1972, 20 U.S.C. § 1281 et seq.
Provides for equal opportunity for women in all facets of education, including
athletics.

Ross* v. *Creighton University, 957 F.2d 410 (1992)
Held that Creighton University could be liable to athlete if it denied him any
meaningful access to the school's academic curriculum.

Freshman Academic Requirements ("Proposition 16"), NCAA Bylaw 14.3
Sets minimum academic standards for athletes to compete in NCAA sports, based
on high school grade point average in core sources, as well as standardized test scores.

Clarification of Intercollegiate Athletics Policy Guidance: The Three-Part Test,
U.S. Department of Education, Office for Civil Rights, (January 16, 1996)
Sets out a three-part test for complying with Title IX: (1) whether women have
athletic opportunities proportionate to the percentage of women in the student
body; (2) whether the school has a history and continuing practice of offering
athletic opportunities to women; and (3) whether the school is accommodating
women's athletic interests.

Cohen* v. *Brown University, 101 F.3d 155 (1st Cir. 1996), cert. denied, 520
U.S. 1186 (1997)
Held that Brown University violated Title IX when it eliminated athletic teams
for both men and women, because men's opportunities outnumbered those for
women.

Cureton* v. *NCAA, 198 F.3d 107 (3rd Cir. 1999)
Held that the NCAA's initial eligibility standards (Proposition 16), which consider
high school GPA and standardized test scores, do not violate African-American
students' rights even though they were more likely to be declared ineligible.

Pederson* v. *Louisiana State University, 213 F.3d 858 (5th Cir. 2000)
Held that Louisiana State University did not demonstrate that female students
were less interested in sports than male students and therefore violated Title IX
by providing too few opportunities to women athletes.

National Wrestling Coaches Association* v. *U.S. Department of Education,
No. 02-72 (Dist. D.C. June 11, 2003)
Upheld Department of Education's Title IX enforcement standards because
they could not be proven to be the cause of universities' decisions to eliminate
wrestling teams.

Concepts and Standards

student-athlete
amateurism
capitalizing on athletic fame
mechanics clause
revenue sports
selective admission
revenue
profit
cross-subsidization
commercialization
initial eligibility
continuing eligibility
fair share
extra benefits

laundry money
point spread
workers' compensation
amateur myth
endorsements
antitrust laws
price-fixing
gender equity
proportionality
Title IX
capping
equal opportunity
quota system

Beginning Legal Research

The goal of POINT/COUNTERPOINT is not only to provide the reader with an introduction to a controversial issue affecting society, but also to encourage the reader to explore the issue more fully. This appendix, then, is meant to serve as a guide to the reader in researching the current state of the law as well as exploring some of the public-policy arguments as to why existing laws should be changed or new laws are needed.

Like many types of research, legal research has become much faster and more accessible with the invention of the Internet. This appendix discusses some of the best starting points, but of course "surfing the Net" will uncover endless additional sources of information—some more reliable than others. Some important sources of law are not yet available on the Internet, but these can generally be found at the larger public and university libraries. Librarians usually are happy to point patrons in the right direction.

The most important source of law in the United States is the Constitution. Originally enacted in 1787, the Constitution outlines the structure of our federal government and sets limits on the types of laws that the federal government and state governments can pass. Through the centuries, a number of amendments have been added to or changed in the Constitution, most notably the first ten amendments, known collectively as the Bill of Rights, which guarantee important civil liberties. Each state also has its own constitution, many of which are similar to the U.S. Constitution. It is important to be familiar with the U.S. Constitution because so many of our laws are affected by its requirements. State constitutions often provide protections of individual rights that are even stronger than those set forth in the U.S. Constitution.

Within the guidelines of the U.S. Constitution, Congress—both the House of Representatives and the Senate—passes bills that are either vetoed or signed into law by the President. After the passage of the law, it becomes part of the United States Code, which is the official compilation of federal laws. The state legislatures use a similar process, in which bills become law when signed by the state's governor. Each state has its own official set of laws, some of which are published by the state and some of which are published by commercial publishers. The U.S. Code and the state codes are an important source of legal research; generally, legislators make efforts to make the language of the law as clear as possible.

However, reading the text of a federal or state law generally provides only part of the picture. In the American system of government, after the legislature passes laws and the executive (U.S. President or state governor) signs them, it is up to the judicial branch of the government, the court system, to interpret the laws and decide whether they violate any provision of the Constitution. At the state level, each state's supreme court has the ultimate authority in determining what a law means and whether or not it violates the state constitution. However, the federal courts—headed by the U.S. Supreme Court—can review state laws and court decisions to determine whether they violate federal laws or the U.S. Constitution. For example, a state court may find that a particular criminal law is valid under the state's constitution, but a federal court may then review the state court's decision and determine that the law is invalid under the U.S. Constitution.

It is important, then, to read court decisions when doing legal research. The Constitution uses language that is intentionally very general—for example, prohibiting "unreasonable searches and seizures" by the police—and court cases often provide more guidance. For example, the U.S. Supreme Court's 2001 decision in *Kyllo* v. *United States* held that scanning the outside of a person's house using a heat sensor to determine whether the person is growing marijuana is unreasonable—*if* it is done without a search warrant secured from a judge. Supreme Court decisions provide the most definitive explanation of the law of the land, and it is therefore important to include these in research. Often, when the Supreme Court has not decided a case on a particular issue, a decision by a federal appeals court or a state supreme court can provide guidance; but just as laws and constitutions can vary from state to state, so can federal courts be split on a particular interpretation of federal law or the U.S. Constitution. For example, federal appeals courts in Louisiana and California may reach opposite conclusions in similar cases.

Lawyers and courts refer to statutes and court decisions through a formal system of citations. Use of these citations reveals which court made the decision (or which legislature passed the statute) and when and enables the reader to locate the statute or court case quickly in a law library. For example, the legendary Supreme Court case *Brown* v. *Board of Education* has the legal citation 347 U.S. 483 (1954). At a law library, this 1954 decision can be found on page 483 of volume 347 of the U.S. Reports, the official collection of the Supreme Court's decisions. Citations can also be helpful in locating court cases on the Internet.

Understanding the current state of the law leads only to a partial understanding of the issues covered by the POINT/COUNTERPOINT series. For a fuller understanding of the issues, it is necessary to look at public-policy arguments that the current state of the law is not adequately addressing the issue. Many groups lobby for new legislation or changes to existing legislation; the National Rifle Association (NRA), for example, lobbies Congress and the state legislatures constantly to make existing gun control laws less restrictive and not to pass additional laws. The NRA and other groups dedicated to various causes might also intervene in pending court cases: a group such as Planned Parenthood might file a brief *amicus curiae* (as "a friend of the court")—called an "amicus brief"—in a lawsuit that could affect abortion rights. Interest groups also use the media to influence public opinion, issuing press releases and frequently appearing in interviews on news programs and talk shows. The books in POINT/COUNTERPOINT list some of the interest groups that are active in the issue at hand, but in each case there are countless other groups working at the local, state, and national levels. It is important to read everything with a critical eye, for sometimes interest groups present information in a way that can be read only to their advantage. The informed reader must always look for bias.

Finding sources of legal information on the Internet is relatively simple thanks to "portal" sites such as FindLaw (*www.findlaw.com*), which provides access to a variety of constitutions, statutes, court opinions, law review articles, news articles, and other resources—including all Supreme Court decisions issued since 1893. Other useful sources of information include the U.S. Government Printing Office (*www.gpo.gov*), which contains a complete copy of the U.S. Code, and the Library of Congress's THOMAS system (*thomas.loc.gov*), which offers access to bills pending before Congress as well as recently passed laws. Of course, the Internet changes every second of every day, so it is best to do some independent searching. Most cases, studies, and opinions that are cited or referred to in public debate can be found online—and *everything* can be found in one library or another.

The Internet can provide a basic understanding of most important legal issues, but not all sources can be found there. To find some documents it is necessary to visit the law library of a university or a public law library; some cities have public law libraries, and many library systems keep legal documents at the main branch. On the following page are some common citation forms.

COMMON CITATION FORMS

Source of Law	Sample Citation	Notes
U.S. Supreme Court	*Employment Division* v. *Smith*, 485 U.S. 660 (1988)	The U.S. Reports is the official record of Supreme Court decisions. There is also an unofficial Supreme Court ("S.Ct.") reporter.
U.S. Court of Appeals	*United States* v. *Lambert*, 695 F.2d 536 (11th Cir.1983)	Appellate cases appear in the Federal Reporter, designated by "F." The 11th Circuit has jurisdiction in Alabama, Florida, and Georgia.
U.S. District Court	*Carillon Importers, Ltd.* v. *Frank Pesce Group, Inc.*, 913 F.Supp. 1559 (S.D.Fla.1996)	Federal trial-level decisions are reported in the Federal Supplement ("F.Supp."). Some states have multiple federal districts; this case originated in the Southern District of Florida.
U.S. Code	Thomas Jefferson Commemoration Commission Act, 36 U.S.C., §149 (2002)	Sometimes the popular names of legislation — names with which the public may be familiar — are included with the U.S. Code citation.
State Supreme Court	*Sterling* v. *Cupp*, 290 Ore. 611, 614, 625 P.2d 123, 126 (1981)	The Oregon Supreme Court decision is reported in both the state's reporter and the Pacific regional reporter.
State statute	Pennsylvania Abortion Control Act of 1982, 18 Pa. Cons. Stat. 3203-3220 (1990)	States use many different citation formats for their statutes.

page:
38: Associated Press, AP
43: Courtesy of the National Center
    for Education Statistics
95: Associated Press, AP

ALAN MARZILLI, of Durham, North Carolina, is an independent consultant working on several ongoing projects for state and federal government agencies and nonprofit organizations. He has spoken about mental health issues in more than twenty states, the District of Columbia, and Puerto Rico; his work includes training mental health administrators, nonprofit management and staff, and people with mental illness and their family members on a wide variety of topics, including effective advocacy, community-based mental health services, and housing. He has written several handbooks and training curricula that are used nationally. He managed statewide and national mental health advocacy programs and worked for several public interest lobbying organizations in Washington, D.C., while studying law at Georgetown University.